Modern Critical Interpretations

Thomas Mann's
The Magic Mountain

Modern Critical Interpretations

These and other titles in preparation

Modern Critical Interpretations

Thomas Mann's
The Magic Mountain

Edited and with an introduction by
Harold Bloom
Sterling Professor of the Humanities
Yale University

Chelsea House Publishers • 1986
New York / New Haven / Philadelphia

Library of Congress Cataloging-in-Publication Data
Main entry under title:
Thomas Mann's The magic mountain.

  Bibliography: p.
  Includes index.
  1. Mann, Thomas, 1875–1955. Zauberberg—Addresses,
essays, lectures. I. Bloom, Harold.
PT2625.A44Z447   1986   833'.912   85-17523
ISBN 0-87754-902-8

833
BLO

Contents

Editor's Note

This volume gathers together what are, in the editor's judgment, the best critical essays yet written on Thomas Mann's *The Magic Mountain*, arranged in the chronological order of their publication. The eight essays, composed over the span of half a century, comprise in themselves a little history of the critical reception of Mann's most celebrated novel.

The editor's introduction breaks with the critical tradition by suggesting that irony and parody, while intentional and central to the book, have been transformed by time into something very different from what they originally seemed to be. Whether the book's strength lies elsewhere, as the introduction suggests, is for each reader to decide.

Hermann J. Weigand's deeply informed study of "Disease" as a dominant trope in *The Magic Mountain* begins the volume's chronological sequence. It is followed here by Erich Heller's lively and properly ironic dialogue, which stands at the opposite end of the spectrum from the stance taken up in the editor's introduction. The major Marxist critic, George Lukács, who is parodied in the novel as the terroristic Jewish Jesuit, Leo Naphta, makes his own ironic response as he goes "in search of bourgeois man" in the story of Hans Castorp.

A new movement in Mann criticism is implicitly chronicled by the remainder of the essays in this volume, published between 1973 and the present. C. E. Williams compares *The Magic Mountain* to Solzhenitsyn's *Cancer Ward*, in what becomes an interesting supplement to Weigand's meditation upon disease, forty years after. T. J. Reed, tracing Mann's complex uses of tradition, delineates the book's evolution from the "satyr-play" of *Death in Venice* to a *Bildungsroman*. Similarly, W. H. Bruford explores the education of Hans Castorp within the German *Bildungsroman* tradition.

Henry Hatfield's retrospective overview of the novel is a grand summary of traditional critical perspectives, and concludes that Mann again had shown "how form can vanquish content." The final essay, by Alexander Nehamas, considers the most important influence upon Mann, that of Nietzsche, and argues that the ultimate effect of Nietzsche upon the novel is to distance the reader from Hans Castorp. This is again at variance with the judgment of the editor's introduction, and so brings this volume back full-circle to what continues as an enigma, the issue of what are the limits of irony (if any) in Mann's central achievement.

Introduction

I always feel a bit bored when critics assign my own work so definitely and completely to the realm of irony and consider me an ironist through and through, without also taking account of the concept of humor.
— Thomas Mann (1953)

I

The author of *The Magic Mountain* insisted that he wished to draw laughter from his reader's heart, rather than an intellectual smile. He has provoked so many intellectual smiles in his exegetes that they have bored us all more than a bit. The irony of irony is that finally it defeats not meaning (as deconstructionist critics insist) but interest, without which we cannot go on reading. Thomas Mann doubtless was what Erich Heller called him, "the ironic German," but rereading *The Magic Mountain* is much more than an experience in irony. Not that the book ever provokes me to laughter. Mann is hardly S. J. Perelman or Philip Roth. Yet it is now more than sixty years since the novel first was published, and the book clearly has mellowed. The irony of one age is never the irony of another, and *The Magic Mountain* seems now a work of gentle high seriousness; as earnest, affectionate, and solid as its admirable hero, Hans Castorp.

That *The Magic Mountain* parodies a host of literary genres and conventions is finely obvious. The effect of Nietzsche upon Mann was very strong, and parody was Nietzsche's answer to the anxieties of influence. Mann evidently did believe that what remained to be done was for art to become its own parody. Presumably that would have redeemed an irony that at bottom may have been mere indecisiveness. Reading the novel now, the common reader scarcely will recognize the parody of romantic convention, and can afford to bypass the endless ambiguities of Mann's late version of romantic irony.

This is not to agree with Erich Heller's ironic conclusion: "Such is our world that sense and meaning have to be disguised—as irony, or as literature, or as both come together: for instance in *The Magic Mountain*." Mann's story now primarily offers neither "meaning" nor irony, but rather a loving representation of past realities, of a European culture forever gone, the culture of Goethe and Freud. A reader in 1985 must experience the book as a historical novel, the cairn of a humanism forever lost, forever longed for. Mann's superb workmanship fashioned the most vivid version we have of a Europe before the catastrophe of the Nazi horror. Where Mann intended parody, the counter-ironies of time and change have produced instead a transformation that today makes *The Magic Mountain* into an immensely poignant study of the nostalgias.

II

Hans Castorp himself now seems to me both a subtler and a more likable representation than he did when I first read the novel, nearly forty years ago. Despite Mann's endorsement of the notion, Castorp is no quester, and pursues no grail or ideal. He is a character of considerable detachment, who will listen with almost equal contentment to the enlightened Settembrini, the terroristic Naphta, or the heroically vitalistic Peeperkorn. His erotic detachment is extraordinary; after seven months he makes love to Clavdia just once, and then avoids any other sexual experience for the rest of his seven-year stay at the sanatorium. If he has a high passion for Clavdia, it nevertheless carries few of the traditional signs of love's torments. Whether his detachment has some root in his having been an orphan since the age of seven is unclear, but essentially he is content to see, to be taught, to absorb.

We do not think of Castorp as weak, and yet his nature seems almost totally free of aggressivity. It is as though the death drive in him does not take its origin in a wounded narcissism. Castorp bears no psychic scars, and probably never will acquire any. Whatever his maker's intentions, he is not in himself ironic, nor does he seem anymore to be a parody of anything or anyone whatsoever. The common reader becomes very fond of Castorp, and even begins to regard him as a kind of Everyman, which he most certainly is not. His true drive is towards self-education, education sought for its own sake alone. Castorp is that ideal student the universities always proclaim yet never find. He is intensely interested in everything, in all possible knowledge, and yet that knowledge is an end in itself. Knowledge is not power for him, whether over himself or over others; it is in no way Faustian.

Despite his passion for hermeticism, Castorp is not striving to become an esoteric adept, whether rationalist like Settembrini or anti-rationalist like Naphta. And though he is fascinated by Peeperkorn as a grand personality and an apostle of vitalism, Castorp is more than content with his own apparent colorlessness, and with his own evasions of his only once-fulfilled desire for Clavdia, representative as she is of the dark eros that mingles sexual love and death. Castorp is a survivor, and I do not believe that we are to foresee him as dying upon the battlefields of World War I. Naphta kills himself, in frustration at lacking the courage to kill Settembrini; Settembrini is broken by his contemplation of Naphta's desperate act; Peeperkorn too is a suicide, unable to bear the onset of impotence. Only Castorp will go on, strengthened and resolute, and possibly will complete his self-transformation from engineer to artist, so as to write a novel not unlike *The Magic Mountain*.

III

What kind of magic is it—what enchantment does the mountain sanatorium possess? At one extreme limit, the book admits the occult, when Castorp's dead cousin, Joachim, appears at the séance:

> There was one more person in the room than before. There in the background, where the red rays lost themselves in gloom, so that the eye scarcely reached thither, between writing-desk and screen, in the doctor's consulting-chair, where in the intermission Elly had been sitting, Joachim sat. It was the Joachim of the last days, with hollow, shadowy cheeks, warrior's beard and full, curling lips. He sat leaning back, one leg crossed over the other. On his wasted face, shaded though it was by his head-covering, was plainly seen the stamp of suffering, the expression of gravity and austerity which had beautified it. Two folds stood on his brow, between the eyes, that lay deep in their bony cavities; but there was no change in the mildness of the great dark orbs, whose quiet friendly gaze sought out Hans Castorp, and him alone. That ancient grievance of the outstanding ears was still to be seen under the head-covering, his extraordinary head-covering, which they could not make out. Cousin Joachim was not in mufti. His sabre seemed to be leaning against his leg, he held the handle, one thought to distinguish something like a pistol-case in his belt. But that was no proper uniform he wore. No colour, no decorations; it had a collar like a *litewka* jacket, and side pockets. Somewhere low down on the breast was a cross. His feet looked large, his legs very thin, they seemed to be bound or wound as for the business of sport more than war. And what was it, this headgear? It seemed as though Joachim had turned an army cook-pot upside-down on his head, and fastened it under his chin with a band. Yet it looked quite properly warlike, like an old-fashioned foot-soldier, perhaps.

By thus making the occult prophetic of what was to come—the uniform and helmet are of World War I—Mann essentially chose, all ironies aside, a mystical theory of time. Many exegetes have noted the book's obsession with the number seven, in all its variants. Others have noted that after Joachim dies, all temporal references disappear from the novel. Castorp forgets his own age, and the length of his own stay on the Magic Mountain. He passes into timelessness:

> How long Joachim had lived here with his cousin, up to the time of his fateful departure, or taken all in all; what had been the date of his going,

> how long he had been gone, when he had come back; how long Hans
> Castorp himself had been up here when his cousin returned and then bade
> time farewell; how long—dismissing Joachim from our calculations—Frau
> Chauchat had been absent; how long, since what date, she had been back
> again (for she did come back); how much mortal time Hans Castorp himself
> had spent in House Berghof by the time she returned; no one asked him
> all these questions, and he probably shrank from asking himself. If they
> had been put to him, he would have tapped his forehead with the tips of
> his fingers, and most certainly not have known—a phenomenon as dis-
> quieting as his incapacity to answer Herr Settembrini, that long-ago first
> evening, when the latter had asked him his age.

The opening words of the novel describe Castorp as "an unassuming young man," but this fellow who seems the apotheosis of the average is of course hermetic and daemonic, marked from birth for singular visions of eternity. *Bildung,* the supposed thematic pattern that the book inherits from Goethe, Stifter, Keller, and others, hardly is possible for Castorp, who does not require the endless cultural instruction nearly everyone else wishes to inflict upon him. He need not develop; he simply unfolds. For he is Primal Man, the Ur-Adam of the Gnostic myth that Mann lovingly expounds in the "Prelude" of his Joseph tetralogy. Indeed, he already is Mann's Joseph, the favored of Heaven.

IV

Much of what Mann intended as memorable value in *The Magic Moun-tain* paradoxically has been lost to time. The social satire, intellectual irony, and sense of cultural crisis are all now quite archaic. Settembrini, Naphta, Peeperkorn, Clavdia, and Joachim all possess an antique charm, a kind of faded aesthetic dignity, parodies of parodies, period pieces, old photographs uncannily right and yet altogether odd. Hans Castorp, as colorless now as he was in 1924, retains his immediacy, his relevance, his disturbing claim upon us. He is not the Nietzschean new man, with-out a superego, but the Nietzschean will-to-interpretation: receptive rather than rapacious, plural rather than unitary, affective rather than indifferent, distanced from rather than abandoned to desire. In some sense, Castorp knows that he himself is an interpretation, knows that he represents neither Schopenhauer's will to live, nor Freud's mingled drives of love and death, but Nietzsche's will to power over the text of life. The implicit questions Castorp is always putting to everyone else in the book are: Who exactly are you, the interpreter, and what power do you seek to gain over my life? Because he puts these questions to us also, with cumulative force, Castorp becomes a representation we cannot evade. Mann, taking leave of his hero, said that Castorp mattered because of his "dream of love," presumably the vision of the chapter "Snow." It was fortunate that Mann, a miraculous artisan, had wrought better than even he himself knew. Castorp is one of those rare fictions who acquire the authority to call our versions of reality into some doubt. The reader, interpreting Castorp, must come to ask herself or himself: What is my dream of love, my erotic illusion, and how does that dream or illusion qualify my own possibilities of unfolding?

Disease

Hermann J. Weigand

The "Zauberberg" ("Magic Mountain") is the epic of disease. I have known more than one reader to take up the book and lay it down again, for fear of contracting tuberculosis through suggestion. If a hundred Anglo-Saxon readers of the "Zauberberg", selected at random, were asked to tell in one sentence what impressed them as its most extraordinary feature, a majority of them would point, I dare say, to the author's infatuation with so macabre a subject. And regardless of literary background they would be inclined to see in this predilection a reflection of the German national temperament.

The student of literature will doubtless do well to be wary of such generalizations. However, in musing on the problem, to what extent Thomas Mann's preoccupation with disease—limited by no means to the "Zauberberg"—may be accounted for by the social factors of race, nationality, and tradition, he may be intrigued by the contrast between Thomas Mann and an equally outstanding literary figure of the Anglo-Saxon world. There is in the preface to Bernard Shaw's "Saint Joan" a sentence written as though aimed at the "Zauberberg" in anticipation of its appearance. "Crime", says Shaw, "like disease, is not interesting: it is something to be done away with by general consent, and that is all about it." A statement so crisp and so final in its uncompromising rationalism that it effectively shuts the door against argument.

Whatever representative significance may attach to Shaw's flatly negative, common-sense attitude toward disease, Thomas Mann, at any rate, is far from standing alone in his own country in finding disease interesting, in endowing it with positive value, and in crediting it with the development of spiritual values that would, but for its agitating influence, have remained dormant. I have already quoted Nietzsche's tes-

From *Thomas Mann's Novel "Der Zauberberg: A Study."* Copyright © 1971 by AMS Press.

timony to this effect, but Nietzsche's point of view, in its turn, rests on an unbroken line of tradition extending back to the threshold of the nineteenth century and beyond it. To an extent it derives authority even from Goethe. Readers of "Wilhelm Meisters Lehrjahre" (1795–6) may remember that the sixth book, containing the Confessions of a Beautiful Soul, opens with a paragraph that squarely credits disease with effecting the spiritual awakening of the purported writer of these confessions:

> Till my eighth year, I was always a healthy child; but of that period I can recollect no more than of the day when I was born. About the beginning of my eighth year, I was seized with a hemorrhage; and from that moment my soul became all feeling, all memory. The smallest circumstances of that accident are yet before my eyes, as if they had occurred but yesterday.

Ten years after the publication of that subtle piece of introspective autobiography the first brief account of the life of Novalis appeared, and it also attributes his extraordinary mental alertness to a severe illness that occurred in his ninth year. Whether this report be based on truth or legend, Novalis himself, at any rate, found disease a fascinating topic for speculation. "Could disease not be a means of higher synthesis?", he asks in one of his diary jottings, written about the dawn of the century, adding: "The more agonizing the pain, the higher the pleasure that lurks within it." In another passage he writes: "Illness is to be numbered among human pleasures along with death." Still again he remarks:

> Illnesses are certainly a most highly important factor of human life, since there are such numberless varieties of them and every human being has to cope with them such a lot. To date we are very imperfectly acquainted with the art of using them. Probably they are the most interesting stimulus and object of our meditation and our activity.

And there is, finally, the following passage, significant for its blending of scientific intuition and religious mysticism:

> All diseases resemble sin in the fact that they are transcendencies. All our diseases are phenomena of a heightened sensitivity that is about to be transformed into higher powers. When man wanted to become God, he sinned. . . .

About the same time when Novalis was engrossed with disease as a theoretical problem, his most intimate friend, Friedrich Schlegel, gave expression to similar views in the second of two letters that form a chapter of his "romantic" novel "Lucinde" (1799). Schlegel tells there how a disease that reduced him to the point of death turned out to be a spiritual experience that lifted his whole being to a higher plane. Speaking of this "Krankheit", he says: "I felt that its mysterious life was fuller and deeper than the common health of the people about me, who struck me rather like dreaming sleep-walkers." And this feeling reaches for him its culmination in an ecstatic anticipation of death:

> And then I now know that death, too, can be felt as beautiful and sweet.
> I understand how the organism, spontaneously formed, can in the fulness
> of all its vigor yearn for dissolution and freedom, and how it can contem-
> plate the thought of the return with joy and attach its hopes to it as to
> the morning sun.

A quarter of a century later it is Heine who gives the widest currency to the association of health with grossness and stupidity, on the one hand, and of disease with distinction, refinement, and spirituality, on the other. And when Hans Castorp confesses to Settembrini that to see stupidity and illness combined in one person constitutes a dilemma for one's feelings, because one naturally assumes a stupid person to be healthy, whereas disease is expected to be found in company with intelligence and refinement, he is unconsciously echoing Heine and at the same time affording an illustration of how the paradoxes of one generation tend to become the platitudes of the next. A few sentences from Heine's "Reisebilder" will make this abundantly clear: "Die Tiroler sind schön, heiter, ehrlich, brav und von unergründlicher Geistesbeschränktheit. Sie sind eine gesunde Menschenrasse, vielleicht weil sie zu dumm sind, um krank sein zu können." ("The Tyrolese are handsome, cheerful, honest, doughty and of inscrutable narrowness of mind. They are a healthy race, perhaps because they are too stupid to be ill.") Or take the way in which Heine contrasts the English with the Italians:

> And as for the pale Italian faces, with the suffering white of their eyes and
> their sickly delicate lips, how silently aristocratic do they seem as com-
> pared to stiff British faces, with their vulgarly ruddy health! The whole
> Italian race is internally sick, and sick people are invariably more refined
> than the robust, for only the sick man is really a man; his limbs have a
> history of suffering, they are spiritualized. I believe that by suffering even
> animals could be made human.

Clearly, this last sentence harks back to Novalis' view that disease is essentially *Steigerung*, the elevation of the organism to a higher plane. Heine brings this same point of view to bear on his interpretation of Christianity. "Our age—and it begins at the cross of Christ—will come to be regarded as a great epoch of disease for humanity," he writes a few years later. That this is not said in summary condemnation but is capable of being taken as a positive appreciation would follow from the value that we have just seen attaching to Heine's use of the terms *Krankheit* and *Gesundheit*. In this context one of Heine's undated jottings is particularly illuminating: "In Christianity man attains to self-consciousness of the spirit through pain.—Illness spiritualizes, even animals." As every student of Heine knows, this is not the whole Heine: his mercurial temperament kept him effectively from championing any one cause consistently. We find him at other times raising the battle-cry of health and affixing the epithet *krank* to everything against which he enters the lists, as when he feels it incumbent upon himself to defend the Flesh against the encroachments of the Spirit. But in this see-saw of shifting values the descriptive tags remain essentially the same. The Christianity that Heine attacks as a disease of the human race is that same Christianity that makes for progressive spiritualization. What the human race needs for the time being, Heine's thought runs, is more Flesh and less Spirit,—the word Spirit being sufficiently indefinite in its connotation to stand for other-worldliness, asceticism, or intellectualism, as the occasion may demand. The epithet *krank* somehow remains associated with the whole realm of *Geist*, including, it is interesting to note, also the creative impulse of the artist. Thus Heine's "Schöpfungslieder"—that superbly witty little aesthetic treatise in disguise—sees all the problems of the creative artist anticipated in the original act of the world's creation, among them the artist's ever-present temptation to plagiarize himself, and reduces the creative impulse itself to the formula:

> Disease may well have been the ground
> In full for that creative urge;
> Creation was my body's purge,
> Creating I've grown sane and sound.

If I have dwelt somewhat longer on Heine, it is not because he is particularly original or profound in his play with the terms *Gesundheit* and *Krankheit*, but rather because every German read and quoted him throughout the nineteenth century. Ever since the days of Novalis it had been common to find disease interesting and to regard it as a vehicle of spiritual growth. One does not have to go far among Heine's contemporaries to find similar ideas expressed by writers of the most varying shades. Grillparzer's poem, "Der Genesene" (1820) contains these significant lines:

> Illness, thou art a gift of God,
> Let him be praised for thee.

Friedrich Hebbel is another who repeatedly testifies to the heightened activity of all his mental faculties during periods of illness. On March 8, 1843 he writes to his common-law wife, Elise Lensing: "Mir geht es, wie du weisst, immer so, dass mein inneres Leben in krankhaften Zuständen nicht abnimmt, sondern sich steigert." ("As you know, it always happens to me that during states of illness my inner life is intensified rather than diminished.") And again in a letter to Elise of October 25 of the same year, he records the observation, "Diseases that in the case of most people reduce all spiritual functions to a stand-still affect me in such a way as to make me evolve and formulate ideas with an almost greater intensity than is my wont when I am well." I am by no means sure whether Hebbel is telling the truth here; his imagination often played his sense of fact false; he may well have written these passages under the influence of romantic theories as to the effect illness ought to produce upon literary genius. However, whether Hebbel imagined it or truly experienced it makes no difference:—the legend derives support from his testimony in either case. I am using the word "legend" here to denote a prevailing mental slant that is absorbed by the individual and passed on uncritically. Such legends arise when opinions that have a strong emotional ingredient and elude the check of accurate testing are given wide currency. The premises upon which a legend rests may be arbitrarily selected and highly distorted elements of fact. They may be such an array of garbled half-truths as to make the effect of a pure fabrication upon one unfamiliar with their social background. The legend itself, however, whatever its relation to fact, is always a significant factor to be reckoned with. By tracing its genesis and development, by charting the momentum of its growth, by delimiting the social group or stratum in which it is current, we may derive the most valuable insight into the spiritual temper of a social group, a nation, or an age. Legends in this sense are the views that prevail in a nation with regard to its own national character and that of its neighbors.

Enough has been said to show that Thomas Mann's preoccupation with disease as a literary theme, in the "Zauberberg", has for its background a well-established legend, closely associated with the German Romantic Movement and running through the whole of the nineteenth century. There is in Germany a body of opinion sponsored, transmitted, augmented, and popularized by many of the most prominent literary figures of the last century to the effect that disease is more than something to be done away with; that it is a fascinating phenomenon and, possibly, a vehicle of evolution; and that it may be one of the distinguishing marks of genius. Familiarity with this legend is part of the literary background of the average cultured German, and Thomas Mann tacitly works on this assumption in developing his theme. Hans Castorp, predisposed by temperament and environment to avoid trenchant thinking, to absorb ideas in a vegetative way rather than by active analysis and criticism, is a perfectly naïve exponent of the legend when he first arrives at Davos, and it takes the bracing contact with the alien mentality of Settembrini to make him rub his eyes and wake up to the fact that there is a point of view wholly at odds with his own, and that it is incumbent upon him to scrutinize the web of his beliefs in the light of reason. Reluctantly he sets about this task. Unskilled as he is in mental gymnastics, he does more listening than talking for a long time, bent upon spying out weaknesses in the humanist's position, and exulting secretly whenever he catches the champion of logic in a contradiction. But Hans Castorp does not confine himself to reasoning. He calls into play his faculty of observation. He pays close attention to a host of empirical data presented by the patients at the Sanatorium, than which there could be no more favorable field for the inductive study of his problem. And reluctantly he has to concede in case after case that there is precious little evidence of any ennobling or spiritualizing influence of disease to be noticed among these folk; that even disregarding the paradoxical aspect of Frau Stöhr's offending presence, these patients are a giddy, frivolous, squirrel-brained lot, thrill-hunters and sensualists without the inhibitions that tend ordinarily to hold the appetites of the healthy in check. Hans Castorp secretly hopes that this picture of things applies only to the lighter cases, to those able to flit about the dining-room and the sun-parlors. But he meets with one disillusionment after another when he begins playing the good Samaritan to all the "moribundi". Case after case presents the same story of frivolity, of vanity, of distraction and coquetry, so far as the women are concerned, and of an absurd clinging to the banal business interests of the world about to be left behind, in case of the men. In not a single case does he find that special *élan*, that spiritual elevation, that transcending serenity of soul which his imagination was wont to associate with the phenomena of disease and dying. All the empirical data are severely negative. Does he concede, then, that they prove the case against him? Is he ready to admit that his whole reverent approach to disease was atavistic and based on romantic tradition? Is he convinced that disease spells deterioration, physical, mental, and moral, and not some indefinable precious value? Convinced, in part; but not wholly persuaded. Observation and logic have, indeed, sobered him. Critical analysis has operated in Hans Castorp's mind as a powerful ferment during these first months at Davos. He would no longer be caught stammering something about the spectacle of disease coupled with stupidity presenting a dilemma for one's feelings. But Hans Castorp has also had experience of a different sort to weight the other side of the scales. He has been experiencing the effects of disease on his own person. He has been awakened, stimulated, raised to a plane of intellectual and emotional intensity compared with which his former life in the "Flachland" appears as a vegetative existence. This awakening is partly the work of disease; and neither the empirical evidence of case study nor the generous rhetoric of the humanist can budge Hans Castorp's intuitive consciousness of the fact of his own transformation. Moreover, there is a transcendental aspect to disease which is out of reach of the attacks levelled by empirical data: The concept of disease is amalgamated in Hans Castorp's mind with that of death; and death, we know, is one of those "Urerlebnisse" out of which the structural tissue of his personality is woven. He experienced death as an ambivalent phenomenon, having besides its indecent a sacred aspect. And just as all reasoning falls short of penetrating to the core of Hans Castorp's experience of death, similarly disease, bound up as it is with that complex, is tinged with that same aura of reverence and sanctity.

Whatever else disease is to Hans Castorp, it is interesting, it is fascinating. Disease takes him out of the beaten path of respectable mediocrity. Disease breaks for him the fetters of traditional thinking and acting. Disease unlocks the door to life, revealing a thousand unexplored paths luring to uncharted, unstandardized experiences in the realms of emotion and intellect. Disease is synonymous with the atmosphere of adventure in the widest sense. Hans Castorp's surrendering to disease has the same symbolic significance as Faust's concluding his pact with the devil. By his decision to place himself under the law of disease (for as a decision, a metaphysical decision, Thomas Mann would have us view it), Hans Castorp renounces security in every sense of the word; he cuts himself off from the safe and the known to face untried situations and unknown perils,—perils that threaten not merely his body but the integrity of his whole mental-moral personality. By embracing the law of disease, Hans Castorp puts himself beyond the pale of the bourgeois law of mental-moral behavior—of the law that hedges the individual about with norms and restrictions and standards for his safety, the law that provides a set of tested rules calculated to lead to comfort and success within a conventionally delimited sphere of aims and pursuits. All this he throws overboard in exchange for the right to ask he knows not what questions as to the Why, the Whence, and the Whither, to try he knows not what new avenues of experience. He cuts loose from all that is tried, sanctioned, and familiar, in obedience to an urge that, while bidding him renounce the world, may well lead him to lose his soul into the bargain. For in embarking on so radical an adventure, the odds are a thousand to one that his personality, caught up in the whirl of unknown forces, will be reduced to a mass of wreckage.

If the miracle does come to pass, if Hans Castorp does save his soul, despite what may be the fate of his body in the shell-torn field, it is because of the spark of genius that proved to be latent in our hero. Long before he has reached the end of his career Hans Castorp has come to realize (as has Thomas Mann with him) that except for an infinitesimal number of favored individuals, the lure of disease as an avenue to life leads to utter destruction. As a matter of fact, even Hans Castorp would have been doomed, had it not been for a counterweight to the lure of adventure so securely fixed in the core of his personality as to safeguard his equilibrium even in the face of the acutest dangers. We have come across this counterweight in his "Urerlebnis" of reverence, of loyalty, of continuity, of responsibility to the past. This "Urerlebnis" had established in Hans Castorp the mental pattern of relating the immediate to the remote, the present to the past, the individual to the continuity represented by the race, and this pattern effectively prevents him from losing himself in the mere quest of new sensation; for it is by correlating his new sensations to his psychic core that he transforms them into experience in the real sense of the word. It is his sense of continuity that turns his "leben" into "erleben". Life for the sake of living is the formula to which the impressionist (in our case: Clavdia Chauchat) subscribes. Hans Castorp is not an impressionist, philosophically speaking, for his formula reads: Life for the sake of experience.

Hans Castorp's surrender to disease is the immediate symbol of that impulse which bids him explore uncharted realms. His sense of continuity is the counterweight that prevents an aimless and destructive scattering of his energies. These two forces, the one centrifugal, the other centripetal, jointly govern his life. It is in the nature of things that the first of these should be more in evidence in the first half of the narrative. If we watch closely we observe that volume one of the "Zauberberg" registers the increasing momentum of Hans Castorp's abandonment to the unknown, while the second volume shows the applying of a curb, gently, almost imperceptibly at times, but none the less steadily. Volume one shows our hero's orbit in the constellation of disease; volume two shows the curve swinging around in the direction of health. Volumes one and two stand in the relation of passion to control, abandonment to restraint, adventure to responsibility. In volume one Hans Castorp is the heir-apparent sowing his wild oats; in volume two he sobers down to consider the problems of "government". For "regieren" (govern) is that symbolic code word which he uses to designate his activity of correlation, as he sits by the waterfall among the columbines and speculates on the

Homo Dei and his place in the cosmos. The word "regieren" occurs some twenty times, as one of the most insistent *Leitmotivs* of volume two. But "regieren" entails responsibility, a sobering up after the intoxicating abandon. Volume one made irresponsibility imperative,—there was always that disciplinarian Settembrini to jerk the tether; but the night of the mardi gras had marked the rupture of that pedagogue-pupil relationship, Hans Castorp was now entirely on his own, and the problem of self-discipline therewith became a factor. Now it is a far cry from the days when Hans Castorp had lumped together "health" and "stupidity", and "disease" and "distinction" respectively, as synonyms. The change of attitude is fully revealed in an exchange of remarks between Hans and Joachim, a few weeks after the mardi gras, when they have just finished listening for the first time to Settembrini and Naphta's verbal fencing. "Oh, you, with your learning!" says Joachim to Hans, "Getting wiser all the time. . . . But we didn't come up here to acquire wisdom. We came to acquire health, to get healthier until we are entirely well . . ." To which Hans Castorp replies summing up the divergence of their points of view,

> Yes, you can say that because you are a soldier, and your existence is purely formal. But it's different with me, I am a civilian, and more or less responsible. . . . You say we did not come up here to get wiser, but healthier, and that is true. But there must be a way of reconciling the two; and if you don't think so, why then you are dividing the world up into two hostile camps, which, I may tell you, is a grievous error, most reprehensible.

What Hans Castorp aims at is clearly a synthesis of the characteristic values of disease and health, in the same way as his approach to life comes to be more and more a synthesis of the ethos of adventure and that of responsibility.

So far our concern with disease has turned on the question of its value. We cannot leave the subject, however, without touching upon the discussion of its nature,—a topic that figures very prominently among the problems of the "Zauberberg". How is disease to be interpreted? Is its primary significance physiological or psychological? Is it caused by disturbing factors that enter the chemico-physical organism from without and are then reflected in symptoms of consciousness, or is the process the reverse of this, supposing that either alternative goes to the heart of the matter? In asking these questions we find ourselves face to face with one of the fundamental questions of philosophy; for it is, of course, none other than the age-old mind-body problem that confronts us here in somewhat specialized form. From time immemorial philosophers have debated whether it is the body that determines the mind or the mind that determines the body. Fortunately for me, I am not concerned here with trying to solve the mind-body problem as such, but only with reviewing briefly the questions raised in connection with it in the "Zauberberg".

A very general observation on Thomas Mann's way of dealing with problems in the "Zauberberg" suggests itself here. Thomas Mann brings the dialectic method to bear upon the general phenomena that he tries to interpret. He weighs one side of a problem against the other with a view to striking a balance between them. We have just seen him employ the antithesis of disease and health in this fashion, and we may expect to meet other instances of this method before we have finished with our study. In the case of the present problem his procedure is the same. Here the dialectic process is dramatized in the characters of the two physicians, Behrens and Krokowski. The therapy of Behrens, the surgeon, presupposes the primacy of the physiological symptom, whereas Krokowski, the psycho-analyst, regards the organic symptom as secondary and ascribes all disease to the devious workings of the libido. The premises of the one are materialistic (chemico-physical), while those of the other are idealistic (psychological). The one stresses material disturbances that affect the organism willy-nilly, whereas the other makes any disturbance contingent upon a willingness of the organism to harbor the enemy; accordingly, the therapeutic efforts of the one are concerned with the body, while the other seeks to influence the psyche directly. The available data, unfortunately, will support opposite conclusions. Hans Castorp's own case illustrates this beautifully. Directly upon his arrival his heart begins to beat faster, and he is in a state of constant excitement without there being anything to motivate his excitement. He puts his hands to his heart with the gesture of a person in love; he experiences violent emotions as to form, but without their customary content. When he hears the door of the dining-room slammed behind his back for the third time, he whispers, with a vehemence all out of proportion to the incident, "I must find out," before he turns to see who is responsible for the disturbance. In due time Hans discovers that he is in love, and now all is well, so to say; for now the erratic beating of his heart has a good and sufficient reason: the body no longer performs "on its own hook", the connection between body and soul has been re-established.

> He could say, without stretching the truth, that such a connection now existed, or was easily induced: he was aware that he felt an emotion to correspond with the action of his heart. He needed only to think of Madame Chauchat—and he did think of her—and lo, he felt within himself the emotion proper to the heartbeats.

This certainly looks like a vindication of the James-Lange theory of the emotions, and would satisfy any psychological behaviorist. It does not satisfy Hans Castorp, however, who promptly establishes a psychological connection between his passion for Clavdia and his adolescent infatuation with his exotic school-mate Przibislaw Hippe, and who, in a moment of tense ecstasy, goes so far as to utter the conviction that what lured him from Hamburg to Davos was none other than the power of his love for Clavdia. But leaving such fanciful perspectives out of account, what reader is there who has not at least a strong suspicion that Hans Castorp's cold during the third week of his stay at Davos was directly induced by his will, however subconsciously, not to be separated from the object of his passion? To explain his fever as a case of shamming would not help things in any way, for his symptoms were demonstrably objective, like those of any other patient. If one were to argue, on the other hand, that the physiological stimulation induced by the Davos atmosphere was the primary factor, and that it was bound to translate itself into emotional terms in one way or another, hence his falling in love, whereupon the hook-up with associated memories (the Przibislaw episode) is effected in due course,—there would be no way of disproving such a point of view, even though it is reasonably clear that the author himself would not subscribe to it. It is just as well, perhaps, not to complicate the picture any further by bringing up an exactly analogous situation and asking precisely *what* was the relation between the adolescent's infatuation with Hippe and the old, calcinated spot on Hans Castorp's lung discovered by Behrens,—for related they are, without any question. Whatever view we incline to, Hans Castorp's is a special case, it will be conceded, and no binding conclusions can be drawn from it with regard to all disease generally or even the specific disease of tuberculosis. Incidentally, Hans submits to both kinds of therapy—the dietetics and the routine prescribed by Behrens and, for a time, a series of special injections; and he also has psycho-analytic conferences with Krokowski; but we fail to see that either method has any visible effect upon the state of his health.

Joachim's case is another illustration of the problem, and the conclusions to be deduced from it are equally ambiguous. Body and soul seem to be decidedly at odds in his case. Seeing the doggedness of his determination to conquer the dread disease by the most punctilious observance of all the rules, we should be guilty of disloyalty towards him if we were to question the sincerity of his will to get well. Every minute of his daily routine is planned with a view to his making himself fit for military service. That his organism fails to respond to so steadfast a will spells tragedy for him. If his quiet zeal in performing his duty wins our sympathy, the gallantry of his final attempt to force the issue elicits our admiration. Despite his heroic struggle he is doomed. The meaning of this outcome in terms of our problem would seem to be, first, that an organic lesion was the primary factor in Joachim's failure; and secondly, that the power of the will over the body has its limits. The matter is not so simple, for all that. While the first of our conclusions seems unassailable in the absence of more complete data, the second may be subjected to further analysis. Was Joachim's will to get well backed by his whole psyche?—that is the question. Or did his heroic way of holding out against certain feminine charms—charms to which part of his self passionately longed to respond—contribute to his undoing, according to the principle of: Heads I win, tails you lose? Was not Joachim all the time a house divided against itself? And did not those elements of his psyche that were ruthlessly overridden by the ruling faction plot a cunning revenge? But instead of trying to develop the implications of these questions ourselves, let us participate in Hans Castorp's musings after he gets the telegram announcing Joachim's return:

> H'm, it's certainly a skin game, it's playing it low down on poor Joachim,— hardly in line with the contentions of idealism. The body triumphs, it wants something different from the soul, and puts it through—a slap in the face of all those lofty-minded people who teach that the body is subordinate to the soul. Seems to me they don't know what they are talking about, because if they were right, a case like this would put the soul in a pretty equivocal light. *Sapienti sat.* I know what I mean. The question I raise is how far they are right when they set the two over against each other; and whether they aren't rather in collusion, playing the same game. That's something that never occurs to the lofty-minded gentry. Not that I am for a moment saying anything against you, Joachim, and your doggedness. You are the soul of honor—but what is honor, is what I want to know, when body and soul play the same game? Is it possible you have not been able to forget a certain refreshing perfume, a tendency to giggle, a swelling bosom, all waiting for you at Frau Stöhr's table?

These musings of Hans Castorp's sound plausible indeed. Psychology has taught us to regard the unity of the self as the expression of a very complex situation. The self is very much like a state in which a number of parties compete for mastery. There is a government, and there is an opposition that may be composed of mutually hostile elements banded together to procure the defeat of the existing régime. Although the governing faction determines the policies, the opposition, while overruled, is not thereby nullified. It remains a vital force, exerting pressure through propaganda, which may be powerful enough to vitiate the policies of the governing party and to paralyze the effectiveness of the executive. It is the same way with the self. There is a conflict of impulses, and some of them are bound to be overruled by others; but the overruled impulses are as real a part of the psyche as those that triumph. And even after a given conflict has been settled by an act of will, all is not serene. The trouble is that the overruled impulses continue to exert pressure upon the self, and if their struggle to turn the tables by legitimate means is unavailing they make themselves felt in other ways. To apply this view to Joachim's case, may we not attribute his failure to sabotage?

Krokowski would undoubtedly do so. According to his philosophy all organic disease is caused by the libido in one way or another. And where does Thomas Mann stand? For all his ironic objectivity, it is evident that he leans more to Krokowski's view than to that of Behrens, and this notwithstanding the fact that we warm to Behrens' immensely likeable personality, while something furtive and slimy attaches to all of Krokowski's works; in fact, I would point to precisely that circumstance in support of my view. Artistic balance requires just such a distribution of accents. This situation has a striking analogy in the pair of pedagogical disputants: Settembrini is lovable, while Naphta grates on our nerves; yet—or rather, for that reason—Settembrini is the rhetorical organ-grinder, whereas Naphta exposes the live nerve of the problem almost every time. Personalities are one thing and ideas another. We may be convinced that there is something dubious and unsavory about Krokowski's interest in disease; we may suspect that his lectures, ostensibly introduced in order to dispel morbid curiosity in his curative methods, are calculated rather to add one more intensely piquant aphrodisiac to the already overcharged erotic atmosphere of the Sanatorium; we may feel that the surreptitious gratification of Krokowski's own libido is the chief end to be served by his rôle of father confessor:—all this may be conceded, and yet he may be closer to an understanding of the relation obtaining between mind and body than a good physiologist and fine surgeon who is a capital fellow besides.

Settembrini loathes Krokowski. But his own point of view at times comes close to that of the psycho-analyst. On one occasion he impulsively refers to disease as "a form of immorality." I say impulsively; for when Hans Castorp tries to pin him down and make him own up to the larger implications of so sweeping a statement, he dodges the issue and launches a tirade on the nefariousness of paradox. The reason for his evasion is obvious: Krokowski too would cheerfully subscribe to the dictum that disease is a form of immorality, but he would do so with an ambiguous smile neutralizing the accent of moral condemnation inherent in the word immorality; for Krokowski's interest in practical morality is nil; whereas Settembrini is interested in psycho-analysis only to the extent to which it can be made to serve the cause of practical morality. That dictum about disease being not merely a result but a form of immorality sinks into Hans Castorp's mind more deeply than its sponsor intended. He tries to apply it to Clavdia's case, and he finds it fits—much to Settembrini's chagrin, if he could have known it, because our hero's passion suffers no diminution in consequence of this insight.

"Disease . . . a form of immorality." There is no question but that Thomas Mann too subscribes to this formula adopted by his hero. Let me mention some specific illustrations of this that come to mind. Readers of "Königliche Hoheit" ("Royal Highness") will recall that the American heiress, Imma Spoelmann, has a very queer lady companion, Gräfin Löwenjoul by name, who has fits of abstraction during which she talks arrant nonsense and insists on being addressed as Frau Meier. There is no doubt but that her insanity has the function of an escape from responsibility, and that it is voluntaristic in essence. She herself refers to it as "the boon". The same interpretation suggests itself with regard to the epileptic fit of Pópow, minutely described in the "Zauberberg". In his lectures Krokowski had characterized epilepsy as the equivalent of love and an orgasm of the brain, and the scene to which we are treated has all the earmarks of such a performance, so that we tacitly subscribe to Krokowski's version. Mann himself, moreover, speaks of epilepsy in very similar terms in a brief essay, dated 1920, where we read with regard to Dostoevsky, among other things, that he was "an epileptic, and the tendency today is to interpret this mystical disease as a form of sexual gratification". Finally, Thomas Mann has recounted an episode of his own life, showing how the desire to escape from an intolerable situation translated itself into physical symptoms sufficiently grave to effect his release. Like every pre-war German found physically fit, he had to report for military training. He submitted to the inevitable at the time when "Buddenbrooks" was in the hands of the publisher, whose decision on the bulky manuscript was awaited with considerable anxiety. But he soon found the yelling of the drill-sergeant, the waste of time, and the insistence on machine-like spotlessness repugnant beyond endurance.

> Only a few weeks had I lived in the barracks atmosphere when my determination to free myself had already assumed a deadly and—as the course of events proved—an irresistible character.

This is Thomas Mann's own way of accounting for the inflammation of the tendons of the ankle which he incurred in learning the goose step and which eventually brought about his discharge. Perhaps only a drill-sergeant would refer to this affliction as a form of immorality, but on the basis of his own account Thomas Mann would concede his right to call it just that. While differing with the drill-sergeant on the ethical aspects of the case, he would agree that his physical infirmity reflected an ineradicable perversity of his nature.

"Disease . . . a form of immorality." Let us ponder the meaning of that phrase a little longer. The emphasis rests, no doubt, upon the word "form". Thomas Mann carefully refrains from saying that disease is a result of immorality, and just as carefully that immorality is a result of disease. Specific cases of disease and immorality would doubtless warrant such a description, but Thomas Mann is concerned with the specific fact as an illustration of a general problem. The general problem is the same if we replace the terms disease and immorality by the more general terms, organic symptom and a state of mind. What is the relation of these two factors in the human economy, Thomas Mann asks himself; and he despairs of expressing their relation in terms of any cause and effect series. The dilemma that results from the attempt to approach the problem through the categories of cause and effect is neatly expressed in the following musings:

> The materialist, son of a philosophy of sheer animal vigor, can never be dissuaded from explaining spirit as a mere phosphorescent product of matter; whereas the idealist, proceeding from the principle of creative hysteria, is inclined, and very readily resolved, to answer the question of primacy in the exactly opposite sense. Take it all in all, there is here nothing less than the old strife over which was first, the chicken or the egg—a strife which assumes its extraordinary complexity from the fact that no egg is thinkable except one laid by a hen, and no hen that has not crept out of a previously postulated egg.

Starting from the assumption that the organic and the psychic are fundamentally different in kind, one can argue until doomsday without bridging the gap between them or demonstrating how phenomena belonging to the one series can translate themselves into terms of the other. One is confronted with the same impasse that blocked Hans Castorp in his attempts to understand how any transition from inorganic matter to organic life could be made logically thinkable.

We are ready to understand, then, that Thomas Mann's use of the word "form" with regard to disease has a special meaning. It is one of the ways he takes to express the conviction that mind and body, spirit and matter, are two manifestations of an underlying reality that encompasses them both. The equation that unites them will forever elude intellectual formulation. Whether, as materialistic monists, we take matter as our starting point, or whether, as idealistic monists, we try to conceive everything in terms of spirit, neither approach will ever succeed in solving the riddles of the universe that have their locus in man, the Homo Dei. So we leave this part of our discussion without having arrived at a positive answer. Nor is the answer negative for that matter; for in so far as it is an answer at all, it "passeth the understanding."

Conversation on *The Magic Mountain*

Erich Heller

I have decided to break the monotony of a monologue which has all the time, and no doubt noticeably, been a disguised conversation—a conversation with myself, with fellow critics, and not least with Thomas Mann. In a letter written exactly one year before his death he said that "Thou com'st in such a questionable shape" had been "only too familiar to me as a manner of addressing myself." It seems appropriate, then, that questions should be asked.

Q: And music. There is the celebrated chapter about Hans Castorp's favorite gramophone records. Are they not all, although only one piece is German, about our great romantic fascinations, above all about death?

A: Yes, romantically played, as if by arrangement with Friedrich Schlegel, on a most advanced electro-technical contraption. The chapter is yet another instance of the extraordinary organization of the novel. Again, it seems to retell the whole story, this time in the guise of meditations on pieces by Verdi, Bizet, Debussy, Gounod, and Schubert.

Q: A strange assortment. The selection not of a musician—

A: —but of a novelist who calls Hans Castorp's great love by the abiding name of Hippe.

Q: Abiding? The love story Thomas Mann tells is about Hans and Clavdia. Hippe is merely a memory. But what's in the name?

A: Death. Pribislav Hippe. Pribislav is a Polish name—like Tadzio in *Death in Venice*; and Hippe is the German for scythe, an instrument which belongs to the medieval image of Death. Clavdia Chauchat, to whom Hans Castorp finally "returns the pencil," which in a first boyish feat of passionate daring he borrowed from the admired schoolmate, is Pribislav Hippe's feminine incarnation. She has his "Kirghiz" eyes and husky voice, and her profound identity with him is sealed by Hans Castorp's blood.

Q: Blood? I can remember no such drama.

A: Can't you? Hans Castorp has been a visitor in the sanatorium for only a few days. One morning he ventures on a first lonely walk into the mountains. As he is lying on a bench by a stream, trying to stop an ominous bleeding at the nose (soon he will be a patient himself), his mind is suddenly invaded by the schoolyard scene with Hippe. The memory of it has the articulate presence of a vision. And only after this experience does Hans Castorp know that he is in love with Clavdia Chauchat. But what is more: it *remains* the same love. The sex does not matter. Think of Hans Castorp's sleepy thoughts when, in extreme danger of falling asleep in the snow, he meditates, without any apparent motivation, upon pencils and genders in French: "*Son crayon!* That means her pencil, not his pencil, in this case; you only say *son* because *crayon* is masculine. The rest is just a silly play on words."

Q: Do you mean to suggest that Hippe is to Clavdia as Proust's Albert is to Marcel's Albertine?

A: There is no need for suggestion. I merely mean what Thomas Mann not only meant but made abundantly clear: that Clavdia is to the young Hans Castorp what Hippe was to the boy Hans Castorp. In neither case is it a passion from which marriages are made. On the contrary, it is the "unreasonable love" which Hans himself, in a conversation with Clavdia, equates with death and calls by the names of *res bina* and *lapis philosophorum*, names he has learned from Naphta, who, however, added to them "the double-sexed *prima materia*." And of Hans's passion for Clavdia Thomas Mann says that it was "a risky and homeless variety of the lovesick folly, mingled frost and fire, like a dangerous fever, or the October air in these altitudes. What it lacked was those emotions which could have bridged the two extremes."

Q: Which two extremes?

A: The two extremes between which romantic love enacts its comedies and tragedies: a definable desire and an indefinably tenuous hope.

Q: That she will yield?

A: That life will yield.

Q: Oh, I remember: yield a meaning rather than a hollow silence. The kind of thing the Flying Dutchman expects of Senta when he sings of the "sinister glow" of which he is not sure whether it is love. No, no, he sings, "it is the longing for salvation." If only he could have it "through such an angel." I daresay you are right, and the sex of the angel makes little difference if it is salvation one wants by it, not children.

A: That is why I said the name of Hans Castorp's abiding love was Hippe. Death. Life is always in danger of obliteration when those two extremes touch each other and the yearning for salvation becomes fused with the desire of the senses. Listen: "The term he had set for his holiday had long since passed. He no longer cared. The thought of returning home did not even occur to him." Why can't he ask her to return with him? Because of external obstacles? These are merely the feeble external symptoms of the inward state of affairs: Hans Castorp does not want a wife; he wants the adventure in permanence, he wants ecstasy as the daily level of living, he wants the bliss which transcends life and lasts forever. It is the romantic variation on death and salvation. Hence he does not even wish to know Clavdia—except biblically. He seeks to preserve that yearning of which Thomas Mann says that it is "the product of defective knowledge," the exciting tension which exists "between two beings who know each other only with their eyes," and "the hysteria of suppressed communications and undeliverable messages." You remember these passages?

Q: I do.

A: You are quite wrong. Forgive the didactic trick. They do not come from *The Magic Mountain*. Of course, they might; but they come from *Death in Venice*. Tadzio or Clavdia—the nature of the passion is the same. You remember how it ends: after Hans Castorp's long and patient waiting—for on the morning following the night of the *mardi gras* Clavdia departed—she comes back to the mountain in the company of Mynheer Peeperkorn.

Q: Senta with the Flying Dutchman.

A: I doubt it. He needs no angel of salvation. She is his mistress, woman to a man. And Hans Castorp's passion all but dissolves. Only now has he outgrown the Hippe love the other name of which is Death. To the slight annoyance of Clavdia he makes friends with Peeperkorn, the big, inarticulate, tottering mystery.

Q: Yet another representative. He represents Life.

A: Without the slightest detriment to his own. Representative or not, admit that as a literary creation he is a surpassing success. Admit— grudgingly, if you like, but admit—that your outburst of a while ago did grave injustice to Thomas Mann on at least one point: you implied that he divests his creatures of their individual existence for the sake of their typicality. It is untrue. Thomas Mann time and again succeeds in achieving the apparently impossible—namely, in squaring Schlegel's literary circle and giving life to seemingly preconceived ideas as if they were naturally conceived children of the imagination; which is only another way of saying that you are wrong in thinking of his ideas as literally "preconceived." They belong to an imaginative order, not an excogitated scheme. Think of Thomas Buddenbrook, or Tony, or Christian! Think of Mynheer Peeperkorn!

Q: Who is a representative of Life.

A: If so, then not without irony. True, he is Dionysus, almost as painted by Rubens, and a colonial Dutch coffee-planter, as unforgettably described by Thomas Mann. But his model is not Life but Art: a poet— Gerhart Hauptmann. Also, he kills himself.

Q: Yes, he kills himself. I remember an extraordinary weapon.

A: Specially constructed for suicide. It is a mechanical imitation of the fangs of a poisonous tropical snake, the engineered semblance of a demon from such a jungle as Gustav Aschenbach saw in his Dionysian nightmare.

Q: An engineered demon—your Friedrich Schlegel would have loved it. But before you draw your representative conclusions from the fact that Life kills itself with a most intelligently and scientifically constructed monster, don't forget that Naphta, unmistakably representative of Mind, also commits suicide—in an act of sheer supererogation. He had never been alive.

A: And is, like Settembrini, dwarfed by the advent of Peeperkorn. They cease to exist in his presence.

Q: Mind dwarfed by Life.

A: Whereas Peeperkorn, in his Dionysian inarticulateness, cuts an excellent figure in the company of his true peers, the mighty mountain cataract and the eagle in the sky. He acknowledges, almost applauds, their great performances like someone who intimately knows what an achievement it is to be a good mountain cataract or a good eagle—a force of nature. Not to be one is to him the deepest humiliation. This is why he must kill himself at the approach of impotence. He fears that the tropical fever from which he suffers will destroy, or has already destroyed, his power of answering, as he calls it, the demands of feeling.

Q: Life without Mind.

A: Your prompting is better than your intention. Life without Mind. Then you also know why Naphta never comes to life: Mind without Life. Peeperkorn's and Naphta's suicides may be Thomas Mann's way of killing his oldest pair of irreconcilable opposites. Neither Life nor Mind can exist the one without the other. "It is impossible to separate Nature from Mind without destroying both Life and Art." Goethe knew that. Thomas Mann comes to know it again after much "*Weltentzweiung*," much "sowing of categorical discord," as Hans Castorp calls the intellectual activities of Naphta and Settembrini—or perhaps of the author of *Meditations of a Nonpolitical Man*.

Q: So it is for the sake of overcoming a "categorical discord" that Dionysus has to be made sick and Priapus impotent? Irony with a vengeance. *Placet experiri*. Yes, it pleases Thomas Mann to experiment. With what? With all the aspects of—did you say, truth? Or did you say that all the aspects together constitute the "hollow silence" of the age? You did speak of "that lucidly handled chaos" of *The Magic Mountain*, where "hardly anything remains itself," and spoke of it with a puzzling undertone of romantic hope.

A: Which reminds me of Novalis's saying that "true anarchy will beget religion, and religion will rise from the chaos of destruction as the glorious founder of a new world." You are wrong in suspecting that I find it easy to share such cataclysmic hopes.

Q: But you do seem to see something positive in that chaos where everything is not itself but something else. Laziness is learning. Living is dying. Love is disease. Music is death. Clavdia is Pribislav. No amount of debate will clarify matters so hopelessly tangled.

A: No amount of debate. As Hans Castorp watches Settembrini's and Naphta's dialectical battles, this is how Thomas Mann describes his feelings: "The principles and points of view constantly trespassed upon one another's domains, there was no end of inner contradictions; and as it became more and more difficult for Hans Castorp's civilian sense of responsibility to make a choice between opposed positions, or even to keep them neatly apart in his mind, so the temptation grew to plunge headforemost into Naphta's 'morally untidy universe.' "—Even in your most biased mood you must at least concede that Thomas Mann is far from being an uncritical supporter of this state of affairs. The passage continues: "It was the universal topsy-turvydom, the world at cross-purposes with itself, the great confusion, which, more than the 'wrong-headedness' of the partner, oppressed the soul of each disputant. And Hans Castorp sensed that this was the true cause of their exasperation." These are not the words of a champion of chaos.

Q: The true cause of my exasperation is the virtuoso literary manner with which Thomas Mann self-consciously creates a "significant" work of art out of the apparently desperate uncertainty concerning the significance of anything. I understand that it is the vaguely sensed meaninglessness of his life which, in the novel, sends Hans Castorp to the Magic Mountain and keeps him there for seven years. This meaninglessness colors every one of his experiences, even his love. But where everything is colored by meaninglessness, of what can anything be truly significant? If I let you go on, you will say in a minute what every single interpreter of *The Magic Mountain* has said: that, among other things, it is a "symbolic novel." And as the book—how did Friedrich Schlegel put it?—"judges itself," *The Magic Mountain* probably says so itself.

A: It does. You may be thinking of Naphta's description of the initiation rites to which a novice is subjected if he wishes fully to enter the community of Freemasons. "Magic pedagogy," "alchemist levitation," "transsubstantiation," "hermetics," and finally the tomb, "the place of corruption" which is also "the receptacle wherein the material is prepared for its final transformation and purification"—these are the terms Naphta uses when he tells Hans Castorp of the mysteries of the mystery religion. It is clear, I think, that they stand at the same time for the education young Castorp receives as the hero of the *Bildungsroman*. And then again: "The way of the mysteries and of the purification . . . leads through the fear of death and the sphere of corruption; and the apprentice, the neophyte, is the spirit of youth in person, guided by shrouded figures who are nothing but the shadows of the mystery." All this, I am sure, is meant to reflect upon the novel itself.

Q: And the most shadowy of the shadows is no doubt Herr Naphta himself, the Nietzschean Jesuit and full-time mouthpiece. Yet I expect that what is meant is the whole shrouded party of Hans Castorp's educators: Settembrini, Behrens, Madame Chauchat, Mynheer Peeperkorn. If these are the shadows of the mystery, pray you, what precisely is the mystery?

A: You don't mean "precisely," do you? Anything may be precise except a mystery. May I remind you of Thomas Mann's very Goethean definition of "symbolic significance"? The occasion is Hans Castorp's growing enchantment with Schubert's song of the linden-tree, and his ever clearer realization of its "meaning." The song acquires great significance for him, and Thomas Mann asks: "In what does the significance of a significant subject lie? In the fact that it points beyond itself, that it is the expression and representation of something general, something universal, of a whole world of thought and feeling. . . ." There is only one "precise" way of describing a mystery, or suggesting a "whole world of thought and feeling": to find their concrete symbols. The passages I have just read out to you are, I think, disguised declarations by the novelist concerning the intention of his novel. Yes, he meant to write a symbolic novel.

Q: You see! I am asking you how anybody can arrive at anything significant in a meaningless world, and you answer: by writing a symbolic novel. Symbolic of what?

A: And what if I said: symbolic of the difficulty of writing a novel, significant of the vital irony of an artist who produces works of art against, and almost from, the ubiquitous suggestion that it is meaningless to produce works of art?

Q: It would not be an answer. It would be a joke.

A: You were polite enough not to laugh when a little while ago I spoke of the *ne plus ultra* of irony in Thomas Mann's literary art from *The Magic Mountain* onward. I really meant the same thing. However, it would be a joke if I meant anything less than a work of art. As I mean a work of art, it is serious. For a work of art is the vindication of meaning.

Q: Even if it is symbolic of meaninglessness?

A: If it is a work of art, it will be in some sense symbolic. If it is symbolic, it can only be symbolic of meaning—although it may say: "The world is meaningless."

Q: We are ourselves approaching the grand confusion, the *quazzabuglio* of Messrs. Naphta and Settembrini. I shall soon be as speechless as young Castorp is on those occasions.

A: And you will *tell* me that you are. "I am speechless," your speech will say. And it will not be unlike a work of art saying: "Everything is meaningless." If it were quite true, it could not be said—not by a work of art. The worst is not, so long as we can say, "This is the worst." There is reason for rejoicing as long as tragedies can be written. The preserved form of a piece of literature gives the marginal lie to the expressed conviction that everything is in a state of dissolution. It is an exceedingly ironical situation—a situation which has found in *The Magic Mountain* its appropriately ironical literary shape. Never before has the falling apart of all things been treated with so intensely conscious an artistic determination to hold them together.

Q: By the arrangement of words on a page?

A: Yes. And therefore as facts of the mind. And therefore as a human reality. If this were not the case, literature would not be worth the paper it is written on. The story of *The Magic Mountain* is, as it were, told twice: once as a series of incidents and experiences, and then again as a series of intimations conveyed through the very shape of the work. The arrangement between the two is not smoothly harmonious, but ironical and contrapuntal, like the two parts, the one Apolline, the other Dionysian, of the dream Hans Castorp has in the snow, the "dream poem of humanity" he composes on the verge of death, which teaches him the true state and status of *Homo Dei*, the lord of all contradictions, "between mystic community and windy individualism." It would be a bad and unconvincing dream had it to rely for its authenticity only on the story told. Its proof is in the telling.

Q: You mean in the form, not in the content? I understand. The form, you mean, tells a story of its own, a story which stands in a contrapuntal relationship to the series of incidents?

A: Yes; and as a *Bildungsroman* it stands in the same ironical relationship to the rules of the genre. Wilhelm Meister, the model hero of such a novel, begins as an *Originalgenie* and ends as a useful member of society. Hans Castorp begins as a useful member of society and ends approaching the state of being an *Originalgenie.*

Q: Yet he eventually leaves the Magic Mountain to do his duty by his country.

A: Which happens to be about to destroy itself in war; and most probably will destroy its citizen Castorp. We catch a last glimpse of him amid the shrapnel of a battlefield in Flanders.

Q: And if he survives?

A: If you insist on playing this literary parlor game, my guess is that he would write a novel.

Q: I agree. With all that hermetic education in him, he cannot possibly go back to being a shipbuilding engineer in Hamburg. So he will be a writer and write a novel—most probably *The Magic Mountain.* The Eternal Recurrence—

A: —will not take place. For here we end our conversation.

Q: It is an unsatisfactory ending—a little *too* ironical. You appear to be saying two things. Firstly, that it is the aim of an education for life to produce writers of fiction; and secondly, that to acquire true identity means to lose one's identity. For you have previously told us that, according to Thomas Mann, the loss of identity is the professional hazard of literary men.

A: "Literature" and "nonidentity" are, in this case, the aesthetic incognito which a man, incapable of accepting a meaningless existence, chooses in a world which insists upon living as if life were meaningless. Kierkegaard meant something similar when he defined irony as the incognito of the moralist.

Q: Why has Kierkegaard's moralist got to use an incognito?

A: "Because he knows that his manner of existing inwardly cannot be expressed in terms of the world." Such is our world that sense and meaning have to be disguised—as irony, or as literature, or as both come together: for instance in *The Magic Mountain.*

In Search of Bourgeois Man

Georg Lukács

The Magic Mountain is devoted to the ideological struggle between life and death, health and sickness, reaction and democracy. With his usual symbolic flair Mann sets these struggles in a Swiss luxury sanatorium. Here then sickness and health, their psychological and moral consequences are not abstract theorems, they are not 'symbolic' in a narrow sense, but grow organically and directly out of the physical, mental and emotional lives of the people living there. Only someone who read the book superficially at the time of its publication could have missed the political and philosophical problems which underlay the rich and fascinating picture of physical illness. A closer look shows that it is just such a *milieu* which can bring out all the dialectical aspects of the problem. But the seclusion of life in the sanatorium has yet a more important artistic function. Mann, like most really good novelists, worries little about details of characterization. He rarely 'invents' them. But he had an infallible instinct for the right kind of story and surroundings, that which would most clearly bring out his particular problem, which would give most scope for pathos and irony. There is always a delightful mingling in his work of a phantastic or semi-phantastic whole and very down-to-earth detail. Thomas Mann was following on here from Chamisso (*Peter Schlemihl*), E. T. A. Hoffmann and Gottfried Keller, but in an altogether original way. Neither in technique nor in use of detail did he resemble them. 'We describe the everyday,' he once said, 'but the everyday becomes strange if it is cultivated on strange foundations.' The small princely court of *Royal Highness* produced just such a semi-phantastic background to the problem of 'composure'. The sanatorium in *The Magic Mountain* does the same.

    The characters are 'on holiday', removed from everyday cares and the struggle for existence. The whole mental, emotional, moral world which they bring with them has a chance to express itself more freely, uninhibitedly, more concentratedly, to open out to the ultimate questions of life. What emerges is a deeply realistic portrayal of the contemporary bourgeois which has its tragi-comic distortions and its moments of phantasy. The inner emptiness, the moral instability knows no bounds and often explodes in the most grotesque forms. On the other hand, the better exemplars become aware of a meaning to life of which they have had no time to think in the everyday world of capitalism.

These are the conditions for the 'educational novel' which deals with an average pre-War German, Hans Castorp. Its main intellectual theme is the symbolical duel between the representatives of light and darkness, the Italian humanist democrat Settembrini and the Jesuit-educated Jew, Naphta, spokesman of a Catholicising, pre-Fascist ideology. These two wage war over the soul of an average German bourgeois.

It is alas impossible in the small compass of these remarks to give any real indication of the richness of these duels, which are intellectual, human, emotional, political, moral and philosophical. We must limit ourselves to the fact that they end in a draw. Hans Castorp, exhausted by his efforts to reach clarity in his political and philosophical thinking, sinks into the mean, mindless, repellent everyday life of the Magic Mountain. For the 'holiday' from material cares has two sides. It may raise one intellectually, but it may also push one down further into the morass of the instincts than would normally have been possible in everyday life 'down below'. People do not gain any new and better faculties in this rarified, half-phantastic milieu. But the faculties they do have acquire much greater definition. Objectively their inner potentialities are not increased. But we see them unartificially through a magnifying glass, in slow motion. It is true that in the end Castorp 'saves' himself from complete submergence by joining the German army in August, 1914. But from the standpoint of German intelligentsia and bourgeoisie, of all those who stood at a crossroads, yet could come to no decision in their 'power-protected inwardness', participation in the war, in word or deed, was, as Ernst Bloch once wittily put it, just 'one more long holiday'.

Thomas Mann's account, then, of the effect of his own new outlook on the mind of the German bourgeois is as sceptical, and justifiably so, as his critique of the anti-democratic ideology is firm. Both themes are developed in *Mario and the Magician*. In between, in *Disorder and Early Sorrow*, Mann gives a nuanced ironical picture of the melancholy preoccupation with death of a typical bourgeois of the pre-war period, who feels intellectually, emotionally and morally forsaken in the Weimar republic, although he is vaguely aware that his attitude is deeply problematic. 'He knows,' Mann wrote of Cornelius, 'that professors of history do not like history for what it is but for what it has been. They hate upheavals in the present because they feel them to be lawless, incoherent and impudent—in a word "unhistorical". Their heart belongs with the coherent, pious and historical past. . . . What has passed is eternal, that is, it is dead. And death is the source of all piety and all traditional values.'

The later *Novelle* is *Mario*, written in the Weimar years. The story takes place in Italy, which is no accident since what we are concerned with here is the mass tactics of fascism, the use of suggestion and hypnosis. The assault on the intellect and the will—this is what the philosophy of militant reaction comes to once it leaves the study and the literary cafés for the streets, when the Schopenhauers and Nietzsches are succeeded by the Hitlers and Rosenbergs. Thomas Mann gives this new phase once more a tangible presence. Again he presents a subtle spectrum of all the different kinds of helplessness with which the German bourgeois faces the hypnotic power of fascism. And again we must content ourselves with one significant example.

A 'gentleman from Rome' refuses to submit to the magician's hypnotic command to dance, only to succumb after a short but tough resistance. Thomas Mann adds a penetrating account of this defeat: 'If I understand what was going on, it was the negative character of the young man's fighting position which was his undoing. It is likely that *not* willing is not a practical state of mind; *not* to want to do something may be in the long run a mental content impossible to subsist on. Between not willing a certain thing and not willing at all, in other words yielding to another person's will, there may lie too small a space for the idea of freedom to squeeze into.' The defencelessness of those German bourgeois who did not want Hitler but who obeyed him for over a decade without demur has never been better described. But what is the reason for this defencelessness?

On one occasion Hans Castorp says of Settembrini, the democrat, 'You are a windbag and a hand-organ man to be sure. But you mean well, you mean much better, and more to my mind than that knife-edged little Jesuit and terrorist, apologist of the Inquisition and the knout, with his round eye-glasses—though he is nearly always right when you and he come to grips over my paltry soul, like God and the Devil in the medieval legends. . . .' Why can Naphta conquer Settembrini in argument? The question receives a clear answer in the novel. At one point, when Castorp is ill, he has a conversation with his tutor in democracy about the capitalist world 'down below'. Castorp sums up his own gloomy moral experience in these words: 'One must be rich down there . . . if you aren't rich, or if you leave off being, then woe be unto you . . . it often struck me that it was pretty strong, as I can see now, though I am a native of the place and for myself have never had to suffer from it. . . . What were the words you used—phlegmatic and energetic. That's very good. But what does it mean? It means hard, cold. And what do hard and cold mean? They mean cruel. It is a cruel atmosphere down there, cruel and ruthless. When you lie here and look at it, from a distance, it makes you shudder.' But Settembrini calls all this sentimentality best left to the 'drones'. He is a harbinger of progress *sans phrase*. He makes no self-criticism, has neither doubts nor reservations, which is why—although he has no personal stake in it—he is such an uncritical standard-bearer of the capitalist system. And that is why he has no really effective intellectual weapons with which to fight Naphta's anti-capitalist demagogy. This brings out perfectly the basic weakness of the average modern bourgeois democratic attitude when faced with a reactionary anti-capitalist demagogy. At the same time it reveals Castorp's own indecision and unwillingness to act, the same pure negativity that we saw in the unavailing resistance of the 'gentleman from Rome'.

Thomas Mann also shows us in his hero the inner social mechanism of the modern German bourgeois psyche. He says of Hans Castorp: 'A man lives not only his personal life, as an individual, but also, consciously or unconsciously, the life of his epoch and his contemporaries. He may regard the general, impersonal foundations of his existence as definitely settled and taken for granted, and be as far from assuming a critical attitude toward them as our good Hans Castorp really was; yet it is quite conceivable that he may none the less be vaguely conscious of the deficiencies of his epoch and find them prejudicial to his own moral well-being. All sorts of personal aims, ends, hopes, prospects, hover before the eyes of the individual, and out of these he derives the impulse to ambition and achievement. How, if the life about him, if his own time seem, however outwardly stimulating, to be at bottom empty of such food for his aspiration; if he privately recognize it to be hopeless, viewless, help-less, opposing only a hollow silence to all the questions man puts, con-sciously or unconsciously, yet somehow puts, as to the final, absolute, and abstract meaning in all his efforts and activities; then, in such a case, a certain laming of the personality is bound to occur, the more inevitably the more upright the character in question; a sort of palsy, as it were, which may even extend from his spiritual and moral over into his physical and organic part. In an age that affords no satisfying answer to the eternal question of "Why?" "To what end?" a man who is capable of achievement over and above the average and expected modicum must be equipped either with a moral remoteness and single-mindedness which is rare indeed and of heroic mould, or else with an exceptionally robust vitality. Hans Castorp had neither the one nor the other of these; and thus he must be considered mediocre, though in an entirely honourable sense.'

In the novel—the quotation occurs near the beginning and traces the previous development of the engineer, who has just graduated—this mediocrity born of the lack of worthwhile aims may indeed be most honourable, even if with a little irony. But when the Castorp type is confronted by the life-and-death questions of his country, he must be judged differently, just as his situation is different. His honourable mediocrity, his apathy, indecision, his powerlessness before Naphta's demagogy, despite his sympathy with Settembrini, are all transformed into historical guilt. The 'gentleman from Rome' was also honourable in his desire to 'fight for the dignity of the human race', but this did not save him. He joined in with the rest of the bacchantes who had yielded up their wills to the fascist hypnosis. And this wild dance was within an ace of becoming the death dance of civilization.

If, therefore, Thomas Mann had really found his German bourgeois in Professor Cornelius, Hans Castorp or the 'gentleman from Rome'; or, rather, if his search had stopped with his masterly portrait of the German bourgeois who tolerated Hitlerism and even took part in its unscrupulous wars and plundering expeditions 'as a good honest soldier', then his works would have ended on a note of pessimism, deeper than that of any other German writer.

It is, therefore, no accident that during the fearful years of Hitler's rule, while the German people degenerated under fascism, Mann wrote his one great historical work, *Lotte in Weimar* (1939). In the giant figure of Goethe he brought together all the best forces in the German bourgeoisie. Goethe is the Gulliver of Lilliputian Weimar, always in doubt but always rescuing himself and perfecting his intellectual, artistic and moral development. For decades Goethe had been the philistine companion of writers and scholars who used him for their fashionable obscurantism. Mann now cleansed his portrait of reactionary filth. While the German bourgeoisie was degrading itself to the utmost, wading in the bloodstained swamp of a drunken barbarism, here was the image of its highest potentialities, of its, doubtless, problematic but also truthful and forward-pointing humanism.

It is only with the deepest reverence and love that one can treat this book. It saved Germany's honour in the hour of its most dreadful degradation. But this novel of Goethe is more than a monumental song of consolation for a drunken people hurling itself nihilistically into the abyss of fascism. It returns to the past in order to give promise for the future. By re-creating the best that German bourgeois culture had achieved, Mann seeks to awaken its buried, aberrant and brutalized potentialities. Mann's appeal rang with a primal moral optimism; what was possible once could always be realized again.

Not an Inn, But an Hospital

C. E. Williams

In the summer of 1912 Thomas Mann paid a visit to his wife who was undergoing a short course of treatment in a Davos sanatorium. His experiences there inspired the idea of writing a humorous counterpoint to the recently completed *Death in Venice*, a satyr play to parody and offset the tragic novella. Before the new work was finished the war intervened and it was not until 1924 that *The Magic Mountain* finally appeared. Out of the ironic novella had grown a massive novel and modern literature acquired one of its major achievements. Mann's book relates the adventures of a pleasant young naval architect from Hamburg who visits his cousin in a sanatorium for three weeks and remains there for a total of seven years. During this time he undertakes an emotional and intellectual odyssey that amply justifies the generic connection with the traditional *Bildungsroman*, or novel of spiritual education. Influenced by various personalities, principles and forces, compelled to come to terms with their arguments and values, Hans Castorp slowly and painfully works out his own salvation and is eventually summoned back to the "flat-lands" of ordinary life by the bugles of August 1914. The novel is the highly organized work of a supremely self-conscious writer who bids us read it at least twice in order to appreciate its complex structure.

It is a far cry from the world of *The Magic Mountain* to that of Solzhenitsyn's *Cancer Ward*—from Edwardian Europe to Russia in the wake of Stalinism, from opulent Davos to provincial Tashkent. Hans Castorp enjoys a private income adequate to sustain an indefinite stay in a private hospital; Solzhenitsyn's principal character Oleg Kostoglotov is a former political prisoner who can barely stretch to a mouthful of shashlik. The dapper young gentleman from Hamburg grapples at leisure

From *Forum for Modern Language Studies* 9, no. 4 (October 1973). Copyright © 1973 by University of St. Andrews, Scotland, Department of French.

with philosophical and metaphysical problems of Death, Time and disease, exorcises a homo-erotic passion of his schooldays, sharpens his wits and generally welcomes the stay in the sanatorium as an escape from humdrum ordinary life. The precise nature and extent of his illness are never unambiguously stated, but it is clear that he is not seriously ill. The scarred, unkempt and bedraggled Kostoglotov is concerned to win a new, if limited lease of life of a kind that is worth living, and to come to terms with his experience of the Soviet system. When *he* enters hospital, he is on the verge of death. Thus the characters, the *mise en scène* and the themes of the two novels could scarcely be more incongruous, despite the obvious common factor of a hospital background. Yet an insignificant parallel sticks in the mind. Kostoglotov serves seven years in the army and spends seven years in labour camps before being released into perpetual exile and the cancer ward—"twice seven years, twice that mythical or biblical term." Hans Castorp for his part spends seven years in the spell of the Magic Mountain and is overtly linked with the *Siebenschläfer* (the seven sleepers or seven-year sleeper) of legend and folklore. As one begins to analyse and assess the two works, further and more interesting parallels come to light.

The Magic Mountain, as I have already noted, is deliberately written in the *Bildungsroman* tradition, the kind of novel that follows its hero's career from childhood to maturity, usually moving from a stage of youthful egoism and irresponsibility to a harmonious integration with society. Yet with Mann the tradition is turned on its head. Hans Castorp's insight is one thing, his ability to act on it another. The saving grace vouchsafed to him in the blizzard, when he glimpses the true relationship between life and death and the outline of a new humanism, fades even by that same evening, like Thomas Buddenbrook's vision in an earlier novel. After running the gauntlet of various emotional experiences and picking his way through the dialectical minefield of his querulous mentors, Hans Castorp still hasn't the strength of will to leave the sanatorium and apply his new-found knowledge in the flat-lands. It takes the outbreak of the First World War to shatter the spell of the Magic Mountain and as we take leave of the hero, he is stumbling across a battlefield through a hail of fire, with his social future distinctly in doubt. No matter, says the narrator, it is not the hero as such, the character for his own sake, who interests us but rather his story, the *Bildung* that he has acquired. When he began his journey of discovery Hans Castorp was a relatively inexperienced young man whose conventionality would be complete but for the three factors that provide a key to subsequent developments: his familiarity with death, his long forgotten feelings for a schoolfriend, and an unconscious dissatisfaction with the pattern of ordinary life which has lost sight of any meaningful goals. Oleg Kostoglotov, on the other hand, is scarred by too much experience. After the war came the camps to which he was condemned as a victim of Stalinist paranoia, violently separated from the girl he loved. In the struggle for survival he has maintained a curious strength and integrity. When he collapses on the threshold of the cancer ward, he has already lived through more than Hans Castorp ever dreamed of. Where lies the parallel? The point is that Kostoglotov too undergoes a process of initiation to life. In its own way *Cancer Ward* too is a *Bildungsroman*. The kind of experiences which Oleg has undergone are calculated not only to temper but also to distort the personality. He has never known true, responsible freedom. His adult life has been spent in uniform, behind barbed wire and for a brief interval in supervised exile. Although he has at various times established meaningful human relationships with fellow prisoners or deportees, his experience of a woman's love was short-lived and he has had to learn to live without it. He has never had a chance to reflect upon or discriminate between his experiences, his moral choices have invariably been forced on him by circumstances. Now his disease leads him into a totally different situation, brings him face to face with two women to whom he is deeply attracted, and gives him an opportunity to clarify and modify his ideas in contact with the doctors and the other patients. What emerges is a process of self-discovery and of initiation into an unfamiliar world. That initiation is not presented in any spirit of facile optimism. If Oleg tastes freedom, love and political debate, it occurs under the sign of the Crab and ends in a recognition of his incapacity to return to an ordinary life. As he sets off for exile in Central Asia his future is as dubious as Hans Castorp's, for his tumour is not cured. Yet his renunciation in itself represents an act of the moral will which cannot be invalidated. He has attained a self-knowledge hitherto denied him—and in this general sense his story is a *Bildungsroman*.

Hans Castorp's spiritual education is accomplished by the process of *Steigerung*, an alchemistic term implying (as the novel explains) purification, concentration and intensification. Under the influence of external forces an originally base matter is purged and transformed into something of a higher order. Thus the hero, relatively callow and conventional to begin with, matures and gains a depth of insight which would have been out of the question in any other context. An obvious index of his development is his response to the influences surrounding him. Initially he is an eager, curious but passive observer. If he has any mental reservations about his interlocutor, he is too polite or diffident to venture any criticism. But gradually he begins to speak his mind and display a degree of verbal dexterity. He shows himself receptive to memorable phrases which he not only makes his own and repeats at opportune moments, but may even turn against their authors. As the novel unfolds, he grows increasingly critical and independent. Settembrini, the threadbare disciple of Voltaire and Rousseau, is the main target of his newfound expertise but the Italian is pedagogue enough to appreciate his pupil's progress. In the febrile atmosphere of the Berghof Hans Castorp's interest is directed towards problems and situations which, as he is the first to admit, he neither would nor could have grappled with "down below." The same principle of *Steigerung* lies behind the medical superintendent's belief that the Alpine air not only helps to bring about cures but also aggravates and brings out into the open any latent weakness or infection. Thus it is that Hans Castorp begins to run a temperature and develops a "petite tache humide" on his lung. So too the experiences of childhood and youth rise to the surface of Hans Castorp's consciousness and assume a new significance.

The principle of *Steigerung* applies finally to the influences brought to bear on Hans Castorp, inasmuch as they are depicted with a vehemence, a clarity and a remorseless logic that are quite extraordinary. The element of caricature which Mann employs allows him to exaggerate the ideological standpoint of his characters and thus emphasise their significance (and dangers) for Hans Castorp's *Bildung*. At the same time the caricatures can be attributed at least in part to the peculiar pressures of the Berghof, for here everything is intensified and polarized. On the one hand there is Settembrini, the articulate and rhetorical humanist, the believer in reason, science, the power of language and democracy, the man who can quell a lunatic with his fearless rational gaze. He is dedicated to progress, to the dignity and beauty of man, to the principles of the French Revolution and the work ethic; among other things he is violently anti-clerical and anti-monarchic. To him disease is a humiliation, an insult to the human spirit, that must be resisted and overcome at all costs. On the other hand there is his opponent Naphta and the cold incisive intellect of a man to whom piety and cruelty are inseparable. Faith not knowledge is his guiding principle. He has a totalitarian mentality whose supreme criterion is the salvation of the soul, interpreted according to his own lights. He manages to appropriate the economic and political arguments of Marxism while avoiding its materialism. For to him the Spirit is the ultimate reality, the body merely a curtain that separates the soul from eternity. The flesh is sinful, corrupt and despicable, its mortification a source of joy and edification. Naphta values obedience, compulsion and bondage as much as Settembrini cherishes liberty, equality and fraternity. The conflict between them is fought out— with the final pathetic exception—on the plane of argument and debate, whereby they vie for Hans Castorp's support which he just as determinedly withholds. However, he is subject to influences other than the purely intellectual. There is the conscientious, dutiful "military" personality of his cousin Joachim who struggles against the odds to return to the colours and preserve his Prussian integrity against the insidious lassitude of the Berghof. There is the mighty "personality" of Mynheer Peeperkorn, with his boundless charisma, his powerful inarticulacy, his elemental vitality and virility, by contrast with whom Settembrini and Naphta are reduced to mere prattlers. And there is the woman in Hans Castorp's life, Clavdia Chauchat, the enigmatic reincarnation of his schoolmate Pribislav Hippe. With her lethargy and carelessness, her lack of poise and tact, her easy morals, she embodies the "infinite advantages of shame" to which so many of the patients succumb. Hans Castorp's love for her, a delicious voluptuous delirium, binds him in one way and another to the sanatorium for years. All these characters (and a host of others) bombard the hero with ideas, impressions and values which he eventually assimilates and transforms into a vision of the good life. It is not difficult to think of them as representatives, as standing for principles whose significance transcends the immediate situation; indeed, the author invites us to consider his novel as a portrait of the European psyche in the early part of this century. This is not to say that they are "mere" symbols. In the ironic and intellectual context of Mann's narrative they are endowed with a rich fictional life.

Solzhenitsyn too chooses a hospital setting to bring together various characters who have precisely the double function of which Mann speaks, the realist and the symbolic. In the overcrowded, dilapidated and ill-equipped wards Kostoglotov makes the acquaintance of men and women whose personalities and principles complement or challenge his own. Where Hans Castorp is depicted as representative of his nation, faced with conflicting influences from East and West and having to overcome his own Romantic past, Oleg can be seen as representative of the Russian people who have been the victims of Stalinism and have seen through the great lie. His fellow-patients are drawn from a cross-section of Soviet society and counterpoint his disillusionment, hatred and insight by voicing their own opinions and ideals. The most oppressive of these is Rusanov, the KGB official whose successful existence is built on power, privilege and status. His contemptuous distaste for the peasants and ordinary people brings out the distance between the party hierarchy and those it is supposed to serve. He and his wife love the People in the abstract, but avoid contact with ordinary citizens whenever possible. He has risen to power by uncritical loyalty, through lies, denunciations and a silken terrorizing of his subordinates. Politically he believes in a kind of original sin which with diligence and persistence he can uncover. This defender of socialism would gladly pay for private medical treatment if it were available. This devoted family man has destroyed neighbouring families without compunction. He is the Stalinist ideologue whose mental and emotional capacities have been stunted and perverted in his attempts to do one man's bidding while furthering his own interests. At another extreme stands Shulubin, the old Bolshevik, who is tortured by the shame of his compromises with the Stalinist terror. He acknowledges that he and thousands like him kept silent simply in order to save their own skins and thereby allowed their actions to be governed by prejudice, ideological catch-phrases, wilful distortions of reason and contradictions of experience. He has not lost faith in socialism—indeed, he significantly appeals to Oleg not to renounce his faith in it despite all he has suffered. Shulubin believes rather that the building of socialism has been oversimplified and its preconditions misconstrued. A change in the means of production, a certain political structure, material prosperity and hatred of the class enemy—such things are an inadequate foundation for a socialist future. More is needed—an "ethical socialism," a religion of love and trust, which sets mutual affection, not a transitory and selfish "happiness," as man's highest goal. Somewhere in the middle of this ideological spectrum stands the young geologist Vadim, with his implicit faith in his country and the system, and his filial admiration for Stalin. His greatest fulfilment is to know that his time is usefully spent and he is determined to spend his last months working on a new theory for discovering ore deposits. Then there is Yefrem, another incurable, a completely apolitical being who has only ever cared about two things—a free life and money in his pocket. This carefree womanizer and spendthrift construction worker is cut down in his prime and driven to survey his past life in a completely new light under the impact of Tolstoy's *What Men Live By*. Responding to the ethical imperative, acknowledging his guilt, he is yet sceptical of the practicability of such a code. Among Solzhenitsyn's other characters it is the doctors whose attitude poses the greatest challenge to the hero. They are committed to saving or prolonging life at all costs and believe that they have a right to dispose of the patient as they see fit, while keeping him in ignorance of his true condition. Oleg resists this view with all the strength and wiliness at his command, in the conviction that it is not the fact but the quality of life that matters and that a man can pay too high a price for merely remaining alive. One of the doctors in particular, Vera Gangart, makes a powerful impression on Kostoglotov with her trust, her gentleness and her spirituality.

Beneath the obvious surface differences such characters reveal marked similarities to Thomas Mann's, or rather to the forces that

Mann's characters "represent." Is not Vadim the socialist equivalent of the Prussian lieutenant Joachim? Do they not share a dominating sense of duty and time well spent, an unquestioning patriotism, a strong resentment against the disruption of their career, a "military" integrity? Do they not also share the limitations of an attitude in which duty tends to become an end in itself rather than a means to an end? Yefrem's carefree life at bottom resembles that of Peeperkorn. True, the one is brought to realise the ethical shortcomings of his simple philosophy, while the other is haunted by *Angst* at the prospect of the failure of his physical self to keep pace with the demands made upon it; here as elsewhere the novelists use rather different methods of exposing their characters' limitations. But in the case of both Yefrem and Peeperkorn sickness betrays the insufficiency of an attitude based solely on physical appetites and private pleasure. For their part the totalitarian Jesuit Naphta and the Stalinist Rusanov are far closer in their ideological perverseness and opportunism than their respective articles of faith might lead one to suspect.

Mann and Solzhenitsyn choose a hospital setting and the onset of sickness and death to bring their "representative" characters face to face with each other and to put their ideas to the test. In both novels the validity of a character's attitude is measured by its ability to sustain him in this extreme situation. Whereas Mann frequently denies his characters insight into the inadequacy of their position, Solzhenitsyn sets in train a process of self-discovery which affects most of his figures to a greater or a lesser extent. Mann, through the mind of Hans Castorp and the narrator's commentary, indicates the one-sidedness, exaggeration or inconsistency in the declamations of Naphta and Settembrini. Moreover, he incorporates paradox and self-contradiction into the very personalities and fate of his figures. Settembrini, for instance, is a cosmopolitan *and* an Italian patriot; he is a pacifist, yet justifies violence in the cause of national liberation; his private fear of death belies the intellectual calmness with which he contemplates it in debate; the disciple of ceaseless striving is condemned by his illness to a life of ineffectual idleness; his much vaunted logic and rhetoric are easily routed by Naphta's relentless intellect; this champion of human dignity is given to importuning the ladies; his faith in the supreme power of mind and reason is offset by his own inevitable surrender to material necessity, the weakness of the flesh, irrational rage and the dubious concept of "honour"; and the self-confessed mentor witnesses his pupil ignoring his advice and submitting to what *he* considers to be the powers of darkness. These contradictions and ironies are all the more significant in that Settembrini's heart is said to be in the right place and Hans Castorp is genuinely grateful for his solicitude and warmth of friendship. (Mann is determined not to let the apostles of light have it all their own way; he refuses to allow his critical

judgement to be clouded by sentiment or appeals for ideological con-
formity, even though he does not shrink from choosing the lesser of two
evils when the political choice is forced on him.) Similarly Naphta is
depicted as a walking oxymoron: a Jewish Jesuit, an ascetic who dwells
amid effeminate luxury, a communist who keeps a servant, a Catholic
Marxist, a Christian who preaches terror and hatred, an icy intellect who
insists on a duel to the death. He divorces faith from ethics, glorifies
murder into a mystic fulfilment, and generally performs breathtaking
feats of mental acrobatics. His suicide in rage and frustration highlights
the dangers of his doom-ridden philosophy. Both these men of learning
and logic are overshadowed by the magnificent inarticulate vitality of
Peeperkorn, yet he too, as we have seen, succumbs to the ironic structure
of the novel. Priapus is sick, his lust for life strangled by fever, and he
too kills himself because he cannot face the prospect of impotence.
Joachim's unthinking zeal again is defeated by the shadow on his lung;
the latter is the outward sign of the questionable ethics of his "military"
demeanour. The moral correlative of his illness is his darwinistic acceptance of war as a necessary purging of the race, his latent anti-semitism,
the ease with which he transfers his diligence to the very different "duty"
of the Berghof routine, showing that the ideal of service is in danger of
becoming an end in itself. And finally Clavdia Chauchat, with her seductive lassitude, her asiatic lethargy, is assigned by virtue of her illness
to the realm of the morbid, the perverse and the illicit; Hans Castorp's
love for her cannot attain a natural fulfilment and must remain a perilous
adventure. They are all sick in one way and another, right down to the
doctors. The consumptive world of the Magic Mountain reflects the insidious disease attacking the civilisation of the flatlands, the disease of
which the hero in his naivety has been unconsciously aware for some
time and which is instrumental in postponing his return to ordinary life.
For he is subject to vague, inarticulate doubts about the ultimate purpose
of his own way of life and that of the community to which he belongs.
The age can no longer provide an adequate answer when the ultimate
aim and meaning of all its hectic activity are questioned; it offers only
a hollow silence in reply to the honest doubter. And the sanatorium
reproduces the image of an age that has lost its bearings as a photographic
negative matches a print. Down below there is febrile energy, restless
effort, the survival of the fittest, order, discipline and decorum; in the
Berghof there is shameless indifference to anything but food, fever and
eroticism, there is indolence, self-indulgence, immorality, neglect of appearance and conduct, apathy and irritability. With the exception of Peeperkorn, the characters are not given any insight into their own insuffi-
ciencies. On the contrary, the disease intensifies their several weaknesses

or obsessions. For although Death stalks the snow-covered peaks, he is greeted by a conspiracy of silence. The patients are protected from morbid thoughts, the dead are removed surreptitiously and those who refuse to be distracted and discuss death in the abstract are not themselves *moribundi*. They are therefore spared the wonderful concentration of the mind imposed on the characters of *Cancer Ward*.

Here in the self-enclosed world of the provincial hospital all previous assumptions are openly questioned and the patients themselves when confronted with pain and death come to realise at least dimly the inadequacy of their erstwhile philosophies. Sickness is the great leveller. The "normal" structure of society is here overturned. The political prisoner and the exile lie side by side with the secret policeman and the camp guard. Their tumours erect an insurmountable barrier between them and their previous existence. Rusanov, tortured by the noise, smells and lights of the public ward, terrified by the thought of what awaits him, loses all his old authority and confidence. His voice now sounds plaintive and self-pitying. Bereft of the status, reputation, influence and contacts which cushioned him in the outside world, he is turned into "eleven stones of hot, white flesh that did not know what tomorrow would bring." In the face of the awful justice meted out to him, he is thrown back on his own resources—only to find that they are wanting. Yefrem too is frightened by his disease. The whole of his life has prepared him for living, not for dying, and he cannot cope with the prospect before him. His savage bitterness is silenced, however, by the questions raised in Tolstoy's fables. (He would never have read them as a healthy man, they would scarcely have meant anything to him; the principle of *Steigerung* is at work here again.) The problems are not solved but the insight which he acquires into his past life opens up a new dimension and paradoxically enriches him at the point of death. The young geologist Vadim, for his part, enters the ward with remarkable self-composure. For the Tolstoyan ethic he substitutes the more concrete socialist imperative of creative work for the collective and immerses himself in science. Yet as his pain grows and his time runs out, these convictions are shaken. His concentration sags, he feels the urge to drop the mask of self-control and howl like a wild animal. Conscientiousness and dedication are, it seems, in themselves an insufficient protection against the fundamental dilemmas of existence. Vadim loses his fatalistic dignity and becomes obsessed with the thought of obtaining the colloidal gold which he believes will save him. In fact he is manifestly doomed whatever happens and his new-found eagerness for life is a pitiable delusion, an evasion of the terrible truth and the problems it poses. And what of Dontsova? The senior radiologist who contracts radiation sickness? The scientific mind who fears to admit to herself the significance of her symptoms? The doctor who once confidently disposed of the life and death of others but who is now herself the object of examination, diagnosis and treatment? She sees the apparatus, routine and human physiology that were once so familiar in a strange new light. Where once order, system and logic prevailed, now subjective emotion disrupts and overwhelms. Where once she was strong, resolute, unyielding, she is now confused and afraid. In a matter of hours her strongest ties loosen and break, the work to which she was so dedicated is effortlessly abandoned, the assumption that she was indispensible is rapidly corrected. As she makes her last round,

> she felt as if she had been deprived of her rights as a doctor, as if she had been disqualified because of some unforgivable act, fortunately not yet announced to the patients. . . . She no longer had the authority to pass verdicts of life and death upon others. In a few days' time she would be lying in a hospital bed, as helpless and as dumb as they were.

One remembers that Hofrat Behrens, the medical superintendent of Mann's sanatorium, has himself been a victim of the disease he now attempts to cure, and still looks less than healthy. Mann's narrator indeed questions whether a doctor who has been in thrall to a disease can ever truly master it thereafter: he posits a certain legacy of ambivalence, confusion, even partisanship that militates against a clear-cut scientific approach. (Again, however, we are faced with the difference between the ironic and the tragic mode.) The point is that Solzhenitsyn's characters are stripped of their customary defences and left "unaccommodated," to face death as best they may. When it comes to the point, the collective is no help or consolation, ideology and reason prove defective crutches. As the author himself explained in an interview:

> Every man has numerous problems which the collective cannot solve; man is a physiological and spiritual entity before he is a member of society.

Materialism, the pursuit of happiness or the desire for life at any price are seen to be false gods, dependent on the fortuitous well-being of the organism. The most shattering realisation is that each man must in the end work out his own salvation; there is no common code, no mutual comfort, no easy appropriation of a neighbour's philosophy. The hand that reaches out in friendship pauses in mid-air, helpless to relieve the other's agony and despair. Nowhere is this bitter truth more movingly depicted than in the relationship between the student Dyoma and the pretty, easy-living girl athlete Asya. Distraught at the news that she must have her breast removed, Asya cannot envisage a life without the physical desirability which she has exploited hitherto.

"What have I got to live for?" she sobbed. Dyoma's experiences, vague as
they were, provided him with an answer to this question, but he couldn't
express it. Even if he could have, Asya's groan was enough to tell him
that neither he, nor anyone, nor anything would be able to convince her.
Her own experience led to only one conclusion: there was nothing to live
for now.

If in *The Magic Mountain* the invitations of the narrator are not
enough, we have the author's own word for it that his novel is a record
of the spiritual and intellectual problems of a whole era. The symbolic
structure of Solzhenitsyn's novel must be more cautiously analysed since
there is no explicit narrative injunction, no authorial interpretation to
guide us. Indeed, in an appearance before the secretariat of the Soviet
Writers Union on 22 September 1967 Solzhenitsyn headed off the ac-
cusation of "symbolism" by pointing to the wealth of grimly realistic
and accurate detail and maintaining that his novel is about cancer "as
such," about what it feels like to suffer from it. Nevertheless the novel
contains several unobtrusive hints that take us beyond the limits of
traditional realism. The author's denials need not discourage us from
pursuing this line of enquiry, for he was concerned to defend himself
against the derogatory implications of the term "symbolism" in Soviet
literary criticism. (There is also the factor of political expediency.) Like
Mann's work *Cancer Ward* operates with all the means of the realist
novel while also assuming the nature of an all-embracing metaphor. The
cross-section of Russian society presented to us is not merely there "for
its own sake"; the setting of the cancer ward is not merely a convenient
device for bringing together diverse elements and exposing their strength
or weakness. Nor is the course of the disease plotted simply for its "intrinsic" interest. Over and above the concrete reality as an extension of
the social world, the cancer ward is a symbolic image, a poetic *Steigerung*
of society. The time is the spring of 1955 that sees the first open signs
of the post-Stalinist thaw. In the doctors' conference room lies an old
copy of the *Oncologist* dated November 7, the anniversary of the Bolshevik revolution. Oleg's first blood transfusion is administered by Vera
Gangart shortly after the anniversary of Stalin's death has just been ignored by *Pravda* in an unprecedented manner. The bottle of fresh blood
bears the actual date of the anniversary and Oleg observes, "Aha, March
5; that'll be just right. . . . That's bound to do us good." At the end of
the novel Oleg reflects, "A man dies from a tumour, so how can a country
survive with growths like labour camps and exiles?" We shall not do
violence to the text, then, if we conclude, looking back over the novel
as a whole, that Stalinism is seen as a malignant growth on the body of
Russia, of socialism and of the revolution. The tumours of the patients

represent the canker that eats into victim and oppressor alike, those who have fallen foul of the system and those who have served or merely accepted it. The image is all the more arresting for the reticence with which these wider implications are suggested.

It would be premature, however, to assume that Stalinism is an inevitable consequence of the socialist vision, for the novel indicates that human evil exists quite independently of ideology and economics. Visiting the local zoo on the day of his discharge, Oleg is struck dumb by the senseless cruelty of some previous visitor who blinded a caged monkey by throwing tobacco in its eyes. There is a scribbled notice recording the incident:

> This unknown man . . . was not described as "anti-humanist" or "an agent of American imperialism"; all it said was that he was evil.

The question "Why?" that burns Oleg's soul as he reflects on this is heard again a few minutes later when he reaches the tiger's cage and sees with hatred its glittering yellow eyes—eyes that remind him of Stalin (the allusion is clear, if indirect). The Stalinist system is implicitly related to the same wanton evil that blinded the monkey, inasmuch as it gave free rein to precisely that element in human nature. The suffering animal is not a "symbol" of Stalin's victims. If it were, the obvious incommensurability would merely produce bathos. On the contrary, the image of the destroyed monkey which still haunts Oleg in the last line of the book stems from a humble, mundane context, far removed from politics. There is a Brechtian "alienation" at work here which instead of making the familiar appear unfamiliar, attempts to make the unthinkable easier to comprehend. The monstrous nature and extent of the crimes committed in Stalin's name defy the human imagination; and human feeling cannot respond to what the mind cannot grasp. The image of the blinded monkey is an "objective correlative," offering the possibility of comprehending that enormity by means of a recognizable analogy. Soviet Communism had set out to eradicate human evil by social and economic revolution, but the end has not been attained and the means themselves have become totally corrupt. The system which has imposed itself on all the characters in the book stands condemned. Is the vision of a truly socialist society thereby dispelled or qualified? Does the novel as a whole invoke some secularized original sin that eludes all attempts at social engineering?

Solzhenitsyn gives no simple or even final answer. What he does indicate is that, whatever its philosophical standing, the stubborn power of evil demands a different political approach from that of the past. If one accepts that the dominant metaphor of the novel has political overtones, then one of the medical themes becomes highly relevant at this point. In the debates between Kostoglotov and his doctors one of the main points at issue is whether life is worth preserving at any price. (We are far from the romantic dilettantism of Hans Castorp or the nihilism of Naphta.) The treatment for cancer is such that it inevitably destroys or damages healthy cells as well as the diseased ones. The problem is to kill the tumour while doing the least amount of harm to the rest of the body. Once Kostoglotov has been freed from pain and moderately restored, he wants to discontinue the treatment even though it is incomplete. He wants to live an ordinary life in peace, if only for a year.

> I am really grateful to you for bringing me into this enjoyable state of health. Now I want to make use of it a little and live. . . . In fact, I don't want to pay too high a price now for the hope of a life some time in the future. I want to depend on the natural defences of the organism.

The problem is made even more acute when subsequently he is given a course of hormone treatment which will render him impotent. The reference to a life in the future occurs elsewhere, when in an argument with Rusanov Oleg accuses ideology of preempting the right of future generations to think things out for themselves; and again when Shulubin, the old Bolshevik and "ethical socialist," denies that one can realistically work for the "happiness of future generations" because no one can predict what their needs and values will be. In other words, the problem of the quality of life and the price one is prepared to pay for it has a relevance to politics as well as medicine. It is a variation on the problem of the relationship between ends and means. To complete the analogy one must consider the second important point at issue between Oleg and his doctors. He reserves the right to dispose of his life as he sees fit and objects to being treated like a child. He demands to know his precise condition, the nature and likely effects of his treatment. He fights against the conspiracy whereby the doctors converse in circumlocutions and euphemisms in the patient's presence, never expressing their real opinion or true feelings. For their part the doctors are convinced that any treatment is justified, provided it saves and prolongs life, and they believe passionately in their right to decide what is best for the patient. Without this right the practice of medicine would become impossible. And again the overt dilemma is echoed on the political plane. The KGB official, reflecting on the elimination of Beria, regrets that anything was made public. Why shake the faith of the people? Why create doubt in their minds? Rusanov also prides himself on his ability to decipher the code of the official press, where truth is revealed only to the initiates who can read between the lines, detect subtle variations and overtones and draw conclusions from the omission, inclusion and layout of certain items. The conspiracy of silence, the circumlocutions and the tutelage thus link the medical and the political spheres. There are no trite answers to the questions thereby raised. Kostoglotov may demand the truth for himself, but when a fellow-patient asks him to translate the words "tumor cordis, casus inoperabilis" on his discharge certificate, Oleg cannot bring himself to shatter the victim's illusions. In turn Dontsova's professional convictions about saving life at any price are challenged by Oleg's persistent criticism. She is aware that doctors are only human, that their knowledge is incomplete and their judgement fallible. For example, they have only recently discovered the long-term effects of indiscriminate radiation therapy, which throw a dubious light on the one-time miracle cure. She herself is implicated in several fateful cases, and her sense of guilt is aggravated by Kostoglotov's protests and appeals. Where once the ends appeared quite clearly to justify the means, the means turn out to have unforeseen consequences that in turn radically modify the ends and cast doubt on the original policy. In medicine, as in politics, it is unwise to draw up in advance a neat equation of cause and effect, a balance of ends and means, for no one can predict with certainty the outcome of any given measure. Yet without some such treatment the patient will clearly die. A parable on politics in the post-Stalin era gradually emerges. There is a canker in the body politic, whether in the form of Stalinism or any other form of human cruelty and greed. And political action directed at controlling or extirpating it cannot be painless. At best it may inflict a measure of suffering and sacrifice even on the healthy elements; at worst it becomes contaminated by the very disease it sets out to cure. Compromise is inevitable. What must be avoided as a certain road to ruin is ideological blindness, a closed mind, self-righteousness and an utter disregard for the immediate consequences of one's actions. What is required is a healthy scepticism towards received ideas, a constructive questioning of one's assumptions, a recognition of the fallibility and limitations of political action, and an alert sense of ethical responsibility which will not readily destroy the immediate future for the sake of uncertain, abstract, long-term goals. And the "patient" too has the right to be informed and consulted if he so desires. It is precisely the attitude which Max Weber characterized as *verantwortungsethisch* in his essay "Politik als Beruf" (1919). The purely ideological or political criterion stands condemned and the criterion of ethical responsibility is rehabilitated, though not at the expense of the political dimension.

There is a point beyond which the parable cannot develop without becoming inconsistent and unhistorical. In a society where even intellectual dissent and ethical criticism constitute a penal offence, the possibilities for depicting any positive political action are limited; conversely the maintenance of ethical integrity, an open acknowledgement of truth and a defence of human dignity are in themselves a meaningful political act. That none of the characters engage in constructive political activity need hardly surprise us, for the situation with which the novel deals cannot be measured by the ordinary yardstick of Western politics. Yet Solzhenitsyn does not appear to succumb to the moral absolutism of Tolstoy's "law of love" and "the law of violence." The ethical socialism of Shulubin which is indeed a Tolstoyan reversal of the existing system and implies that under the "law of violence" the only respectable political role is that of victim—this is not the final message of the novel. Nor is Kostoglotov's renunciation the ultimate *political* statement of the book. Rather we are left with something less "Russian" and more pragmatic. It is an appeal—even against the odds—for a humane, responsible activism which emerges piecemeal from the individual contributions of Kostoglotov, Shulubin, the doctors and the *komendant* who stamps Oleg's discharge papers. And in the figure of the student Dyoma, whose experiences have indeed provided him with a sense of what makes life worth living, there is a suggestion of a better future, at the price of the amputation of the diseased limb that links him with the past.

The Uses of Tradition

T. J. Reed

Der Zauberberg (The Magic Mountain) is Thomas Mann's most complex creation. It is the summa of his life, thought, and technical achievement to the age of fifty. It is spiritual autobiography, confession and apologia, an intricate allegory, a kind of historical novel, an analysis of Man and a declaration of principle for practical humanism. In appearance it is a parody of the German *Bildungsroman*, the novel of education in which everything—characters, action, and material environment—acts primarily to form the hero's character. In reality it is a *Bildungsroman* in good earnest.

This is not a contradiction. Parody and playfulness result almost inevitably when an old literary formula is reused by a self-conscious modern writer. But in *Der Zauberberg* the playfulness is superficial, it is the ironist's gesture of sophistication which leaves him free to use the form he needs. The meeting of recurrent needs from the storehouse of its possibilities is the benevolent function of literary tradition.

The writer's need is not, however, abstractly literary. He did not, that is, choose to exploit this most traditional of German forms simply as a means to make more art. To no literary form is the purely aesthetic approach less adequate than to the *Bildungsroman*. The great examples in the genre—Goethe's *Wilhelm Meister*, Keller's *Der grüne Heinrich*— are records of a growth in their authors' understanding of life intimately linked with their own personal history. The development they achieved and especially the price they were aware of having paid for it compelled the literary record. So it was with Thomas Mann. *Der Zauberberg* is, as he said, a fragment of a greater whole, his life's work, indeed of the life and personality themselves. True, it also aspires to the timelessness and self-sufficient perfection of art. But these qualities and the serenity they imply are themselves part of the achievement which the novel records. The breadth of vision it contains was hard won; the aesthetic freedom with which it treats ideologies rests on Mann's own progress beyond them, not on the indifference and powerlessness of ideology as such. Hence to say that 'the ideologies ... mean nothing as far as Thomas Mann's own beliefs are concerned' is to make the novel too trivial, too easy. They mean what our past involvements mean to us. To speak of them as 'intellectual pawns ... to be pushed about for the sake of the composition' ignores the question which is vital to the reality of a *Bildungsroman*, namely, why this composition demanded to be composed in the first place.

In the very first place, *Der Zauberberg* was not a *Bildungsroman* at all. To understand how it became one is to penetrate deep into the form and meaning of the finished novel, tracing the educative process it eventually describes. The moral and artistic issues of *Der Tod in Venedig* ("Death in Venice") proved to be fully comprehensible only in the light of its genesis; and that was a brief work, written in scarcely more than a year, a year of peace, so that the story's evolution was an internal matter between the writer as a moral and artistic personality and his chosen material. In the case of *Der Zauberberg*, twelve years, a world war, deeply painful personal conflict, a revolution, and the turbulent beginnings of the Weimar Republic all intervened between conception and completion. No wonder Mann speaks in the *Vorsatz* to his novel of the 'extreme pastness' of its action, left behind on the far side of 'a certain turning-point and frontier deeply cleaving life and consciousness'.

The material of *Der Zauberberg* is accordingly change, and compound change. For the story in its very first conception already set out to portray change. Then changes in the external world immensely broadened the issues Mann wished to treat. He tried to work them out in the *Betrachtungen eines Unpolitischen* (*Reflections of a Nonpolitical Man*), realizing that the novel would otherwise be 'intolerably overloaded'; the *Betrachtungen* show an apparently made-up mind. But he then began to change his mind about the matters his broader conception now encompassed, so that, instead of being able to refer back to a definitive treatment of the novel's themes, he eventually had to reject, relativize, and alter the import of his war book, drawing on it as material to the point where its 'unburdening' function was nullified. It is in this way, more complex than Mann originally intended, that the two books belong together.

But in its very beginnings, *Der Zauberberg* belongs with a quite different predecessor, *Der Tod in Venedig*, for it was conceived as a counterpart to the Venetian *Novelle*. Thomas Mann's visit to Davos, where his wife Katja was being treated for a lung complaint and where a specialist, with a 'profitable smile', declared Mann himself a tuberculosis sufferer in need of a prolonged stay, fell in May and June 1912, immediately before *Der Tod in Venedig* was completed. Escaping from the mountains, Mann tried to resume work on *Felix Krull*, but evidently without much success. A year later he had again abandoned it in favour of a further *Novelle*.

As yet there is no hint of any *Bildungsroman*. What then was the point of the *Novelle* conception, and in what way did it already set out to portray change? In two later accounts, Mann spells out the parallel between *Der Tod in Venedig* and the 'humorous pendant', the 'satyr-play after the tragedy', which was how he saw his new story. Both works were to show the fascination with death and the triumph of disorder ('extreme disorder' or 'intoxicating disorder') over a life devoted to order. The tragic conflict and Dionysian intoxication in Aschenbach was to be echoed in the comic conflict of bourgeois respectability and macabre adventures. As yet it was not clear how it would end, but something would no doubt turn up.

What sort of change does this imply? Not the formation of a character, but its grotesquely comic undermining; not *Bildung* but, so to speak, *Entbildung*. And it is worth trying for once to read *Der Zauberberg* in this way, as the satyr-play originally planned, forgetting for a while its prestige as a novel of ideas. The lines of such a conception are still clear in the final text, and they are remarkably close (as Greek satyr-plays are sometimes thought to have been) to the lines of the tragic version, *Der Tod in Venedig*.

Both heroes begin by planning a brief interlude in their orderly lives, intending to return refreshed but essentially unchanged. Both find themselves in an enclosed but cosmopolitan society and are disoriented by climatic and cultural influences and meetings with strange, even grotesque characters. Neither succeeds in escaping from the fateful milieu, though both are warned and consider or attempt it. They are held fast by a passion which is contrary in different ways to reason and conscience and therefore not avowed by their conscious minds, in each case for an exotic (Slavonic) beloved whom they live near yet only worship from a distance. Both find a perverse pleasure in their heightened state, psychological or physical, and the dissolute feelings which accompany it. Both finally admit they are in love and become the willing victims of intoxication, actually resisting being sobered down. Both are accompanied in their progress by Mercury, Aschenbach by the god in his various disguises, Hans Castorp by the rise and fall of 'Merkurius' in his thermometer. Aschenbach finally dies, Hans Castorp . . . but when the end of Hans

Castorp's story comes to be decided, the satyr-play has long grown into something very different.

These striking similarities of motif are not all. There is a more fundamental coherence underlying each protagonist's experiences. A humorous manner may have replaced the tragic tones of *Der Tod in Venedig*, but there is the same suggestion that the hero has a 'fate'. It is conveyed by means which are again familiar from the Venice story. Simple statements take on the ominous ring of potential dramatic ironies. The narrator records Hans Castorp's intention 'to return as entirely the man he was when he set out', but then reflects how far his simple hero has left his native town and native order behind him and below him, and wonders whether it was quite wise to travel straight into these 'extreme regions' with no intermediate stopping-places to help him acclimatize. Through these mild double meanings he is already winking at the reader. And when he tells how Hans Castorp declares himself 'entirely healthy, thank goodness', or when he reflects in his own person how indubitably—indubitably?—normal a product of North German life Hans Castorp is, the reader senses a gleeful rubbing of hands at complications to come.

Or there are those self-defeatingly straightforward explanations of cause and motive, used to hint at the true ones. In particular 'chance' is again mentioned in order to suggest its opposite. Is it really by chance that Hans Castorp looks across at Clawdia Chauchat while refusing Settembrini's advice to leave the mountain after only one day? Or that he and Joachim run into Behrens just when Hans Castorp is thinking of asking for a check-up?

Der Tod in Venedig created a similar sense that Aschenbach's course was a fated one. This was not meant with surface literalism: 'fate' was not really an outside agency as in Greek tragedy, and the figures along Aschenbach's route to death were not really 'sent to fetch' him. They were the formal means by which the modern writer chose to externalize the character's inner decline, especially his slackened will. When Aschenbach rejoices at the misdirection of his luggage, or ecstatically welcomes the cholera epidemic as an aberration of the outside world to match and abet his own, he is acquiescing in what, by this very attitude, becomes his fate. He lives his life forwards, creating it in response to what he encounters. It is his author who views it in the light of its ending as complete and 'fated'.

But if *Der Tod in Venedig* used the idea of fate to externalize a moral process, what was to be the meaning of Hans Castorp's fate? Was it to be merely a comic echo of Aschenbach's?

The humour is not that gratuitous. The inner precariousness to which Hans Castorp's fate points was meant to be a general truth: even

North German normality has in it the seeds of abnormality, just as an artist's public dignity has in it the seeds of aberration and downfall. The satyr-play would have clearly been a *tour de force*: how much more piquant it would be to bring out the abnormality lurking in a healthily 'mediocre' young man, blond and correct, than to go on presenting the tediously familiar abnormality of 'outsiders' and artists.

True, even Thomas Mann cannot conjure abnormality out of thin air. Hans Castorp turns out to have a past which is not quite 'mediocre', although it takes an effort of his memory and the aid of an X-ray machine to uncover it. His family proves to have a history of tuberculosis and his early contacts with death have impressed him deeply. His lungs bear traces of old infection, and his stay on the mountain activates a latent tendency.

This process needs to be traced carefully. With the technique evolved in *Der Tod in Venedig*, Mann keeps up a teasing ambiguity about causes. Thus, when Behrens has examined Hans Castorp, he gives the materialistic explanation that the mountain climate can be 'good for' the disease, can develop it as well as cure it. But for his psychoanalytic assistant, Krokowski, all organic processes are secondary, a view which is epitomized in his lecture course on love as a cause of disease.

Infatuation with Clawdia Chauchat is what keeps Hans Castorp on the mountain. His peculiar physiological state makes him think of leaving after only one day, but when Settembrini suggests this, he turns the idea down with the objection Joachim has already made: how can one judge after the first day? As he says this, his glance wanders 'by chance' to where Clawdia stands in the next room. What or whom does she remind him of? He remembers on the following day, when he asserts a visitor's freedom from Berghof routine and takes an energetic walk, to try and get back to normal. He suffers a violent nosebleed and during it has a memory breakthrough: Clawdia reminds him of Pribislaw Hippe, the schoolmate he was once so strangely attracted by. Returning to the Berghof, a 'different chap' indeed, he hears Krokowski's lecture, sitting (chance again) behind Clawdia.

From this point on, it is plain sailing. Repressed love determines his actions and, by implication, his physical state. He seems to produce the symptoms needed to keep him on the mountain because he needs them. Certainly, he is excited to have a temperature and as he waits to announce it to Joachim he smiles, as if to somebody in particular. A lowered temperature puts him in two minds about whether after all to keep his appointment for an examination by Behrens. But a smile across the room from Clawdia's 'Pribislaw eyes' seems to say, 'It is time—well, are you going?' He goes. When his infection is confirmed he is filled with fear and alarm but also with joy and hope. He can stay, the world of objective fact has fitted in with his passion—as it did with Aschenbach's. Clawdia will go on determining his physical state. She is the mistress of his temperature before she is of anything more, and the lowering effect of a snub from her can only be offset by a successful exchange of 'good morning', which makes his temperature soar again.

Despite all this, we are free up to a certain point to accept the Behrens view, and to see Hans Castorp's emotions contrariwise as the product of his infection (the erotically intensifying effect of sanatorium life is a minor theme of the book). We can even reject the link Hans Castorp makes between the old patches on his lungs and his love for Pribislaw Hippe, although we cannot so easily dispose of the link he makes between Hippe and Clawdia, since their resemblance makes it a psychic reality for him. We can object that the physiological reactions to high altitude began before he ever saw Clawdia. But these objections, besides going arguably against the grain of the narrative, can be accommodated in the 'fate' view of Hans Castorp's adventures. For in the decisive conversation with Clawdia during the Shrove Tuesday festivities, he not only tells her about Hippe, he not only interprets his disease as 'really' his love for her, he also declares that love was what brought him to the mountain. Madness, says Clawdia. But Hans Castorp has the last word. What is love if not madness, a forbidden thing, an adventure with evil?

In this light, all the material and physical causes which have been put forward, and even the overt plot-motive of Hans Castorp's visit to his cousin Joachim, are overridden by a coherent pattern of 'fate' which echoes that of *Der Tod in Venedig*. Doubtless it is no more meant to be taken literally than that one was. But the parallel between the two conceptions is made complete. The limitations of the original *Zauberberg* plan are clearly marked.

But in the *Bildungsroman* which *Der Zauberberg* is, Clawdia and Hans Castorp's love for her are not the ultimate cause of his adventures, whatever he may say. They are enclosed within a yet more 'ultimate' explanation, provided by the narrator's authority at an early stage. Whatever the individual's private hopes and ambitions, we are told, they will not be enough to motivate an active life if the age in which he lives cannot tell him what the sense of his activity is, if the age itself lacks hopes and prospects. The 'laming' effect of the age's 'hollow silence' will actually affect the individual's 'organic part' via his spiritual and moral life. And even a person as unaware and uncritical as Hans Castorp will address those basic questions to his time, albeit unconsciously.

This seems a radically different conception from the one we have been tracing. On the one hand, a narrative which implied that disease sprang essentially from emotions, which traced a spiritually adventurous destiny back to the search for erotic fulfilment, and the hero's erotic tastes back to a boyhood episode, finally allowing him to see his unconscious search as the real motive for his actions. On the other hand, an assertion that the real cause of his disease lay in the constitution of the age, getting at his physical via his unsatisfied spiritual part.

The two are compatible, but only just. The first explanation is deeply rooted in the story and was probably the basis of the satyr-play conception, but there is nothing to stop its being seen as only Hans Castorp's view. What then of Hippe, and the way he anticipates Clawdia, and the patches he left (if it was he) on Hans Castorp's lungs? Well, one has to say that even at that early stage in his life, Hans Castorp's proneness to the disease was already the result of the times working on his 'organic' via his 'spiritual' being. Any idea that love for Hippe actually caused the disease and Hans Castorp's adventures is ousted by the new declaration of suprapersonal causes. We have moved from a Freudian theory of childhood eroticism and of repression creating disease to an even more non-materialistic (and implausible) one that individuals can get T.B. because the time is out of joint, even if they are neither aware nor critical of its being so. This change is an obvious extension of the art of ambivalence, in that one more layer of meaning is added beneath the existing ones. But the addition, apart from its implausibility, strains the capacity of that technique to keep the different layers compatible.

The strained relationship between the narrative and its new ultimate meaning is emphasized rather than eased when that meaning is restated. Hans Castorp has now become a resident and is giving himself up to the intoxication of love, with no desire to escape from it. At this advanced point of the Clawdia-motivated action the narrator might well feel the need to remind us of the suprapersonal meaning his plot now has. He duly interposes some remarks on Hans Castorp's love. It is composed, he says, of extremes with no link of warmer personal feeling between them. There is basic passion for Clawdia's body and there is also something scarcely tangible, 'something extremely fleeting and extended, an idea, no, a dream, the alarming and boundlessly alluring dream of a young man whose definite albeit unconsciously asked questions had been met only by a hollow silence.' And he adds the opinion that Hans Castorp would not have stayed even the originally planned three weeks, had it not been for the lack of a satisfying explanation of the sense and purpose of life—a private opinion, he stresses. It seems excessive caution in a narrator to claim no more authority for his opinion than anyone else, and no doubt the circumlocution is ironic. But it also aptly reflects the way an original narrative is being moulded to carry a new meaning.

Is it perhaps arbitrary to pick out a new ultimate meaning within a single finished text? Two considerations make it less so. First, the exactness with which we can trace a self-sufficient first conception in which the influence of the age had as yet no place. Second, the virtual certainty that the passages just quoted were written with bènefit of hindsight, at the earliest when the 1914 war broke out, perhaps not until after its end had shown a Europe changed for good whose pre-war form had therefore 'had no prospects'. This, in the context of a pre-1914 fictional world, could be stated 'prophetically', as something which even a simple man's psychophysical antennae could pick up. Hans Castorp's fate has become the means to present something far more serious and elevated than the sardonic message that abnormality is latent even in normal young men.

In other words, this was one of the changes which mark the growth of *Der Zauberberg* from the humorous sequel of *Der Tod in Venedig* to all those other things which it also is.

It is time to start seeing what the war did to Mann's work in progress. The last chapter showed what it did to his thinking, and the two processes are closely related. But two other obvious things apply to the work. First, the war gave it an ending. 'Something would turn up.' Something had, with a vengeance. Thomas Mann quickly saw that war would bring Hans Castorp down from the mountain. But the war also disturbed Mann's mood for creative writing, and then destroyed it altogether when it involved him in ever more bitter controversy and the massive task of writing the *Betrachtungen*. He had tried till then to continue with his story, but from November 1915 he added nothing more until after the war was over.

But that does not leave a complete gap, thanks to the close relationship between *Der Zauberberg* and Mann's war thoughts. This means not only that there is much reference back from the novel to the war writings; it means also that one can trace in those writings the changing conception of the novel he was prevented from actually composing. If the *Betrachtungen* text was meant to keep the novel from being intellectually overloaded, it follows that it records the angle from which the novel's themes were to be treated. So the *Betrachtungen* and the accompanying wartime letters show us what the novel might have looked like had Thomas Mann been free to complete and publish it in those years.

In his letter to Paul Amann of 3 August 1915 he says:

> Before the war I had begun a longish tale, set in the mountains, in a T.B. sanatorium—a story with basically pedagogical-political intentions, in which a young man has to come to terms with the most seductive power, death, and is led in a comical and spine-chilling way through the spiritual antitheses of humanitarian and Romantic attitudes, progress and reaction, health and disease, but more for their intrinsic interest, for the sake of knowing about them, than with a view to decision. The spirit of the whole thing is humorous-nihilistic, and the tendency on the whole is rather towards sympathy with death. 'The Magic Mountain', it is called, it has something of Rip Van Winkle for whom seven years pass like seven days, and the ending, the resolution—I see no alternative to the outbreak of war.

The satyr-play is plainly still there in this report, but overlaid by other elements. Death as the 'most seductive power', the 'comical and spine-chilling' effect of Hans Castorp's experiences, the 'humorous-nihilistic spirit' of the whole: so much is familiar. But if all this could just conceivably be connected with some (rather sardonic) 'pedagogical' intentions, it is hard to see how these could have been from the first political. This extension of their meaning was surely the war's doing. When Mann later wrote that he was aware 'early' of the 'dangerous richness of reference' his story potentially had, he was surely referring to an awareness which war brought. The letter to Amann is not simply, as it purports to be, a description of the work as it was before the war, but an account of broader meanings he can now see in it in the light of recent experience. He can call his intentions 'basically' political in much the same way as he could interpret *Tonio Kröger*, under the pressures of war, as a piece of political conservatism. Literary themes, that is, acquire the connotations of political issues with which they seem congruent. Specifically, the antithesis of health and disease on which the story was certainly based has two new antithetical pairs pressed into relation with it: 'humanitarian and Romantic attitudes', 'progress and reaction'. Why? Because this is a Thomas Mann who has been taking issue with the accusations of Germany's rationalistic, progressive enemies and inner critics, and has defiantly accepted their terms while inverting their values. Romanticism as the higher art born of disease, and reaction as a less facile outlook on life are opposed to humanitarian commitment and shallow progressivism.

Now, because a story is a work of art and not a pamphlet, its essence can still be called a matter of intrinsic interest rather than decision. But the 'nihilistic humour' of the original plan, which showed a deepening of the mediocre individual by contact with death, could well be described as tending towards a 'sympathy with death'. And this motif could accommodate a sympathy with the newly associated terms romanticism and reaction, which had political implications. If not a polemical decisiveness, this conception had at least a firm basic attitude. But it is worth noting that 'sympathy with death' is given as the tendency of the work, not yet (or not explicitly) as the preference of the hero. He, after all, is merely being exposed experimentally to that 'most seductive power'.

In March 1917, again in a letter to Paul Amann, Mann digresses from gloomy musings on the future to mention *Der Zauberberg*:

> But I still find it remarkable that before the war, which I did not believe possible, I had politics, and the political problems of the war at that, in my blood and in my mind: the novel in which I was interrupted had a pedagogical-political main motif; a young man was placed between an advocate of 'work and progress', a disciple of Carducci, eloquent in the Latin manner—and a desperate clever reactionary—in Davos, where an unvirtuous sympathy with death holds him fast ... Do you see? And I must write the *Betrachtungen* simply because, as a result of the war, the novel would otherwise have been intellectually intolerably overloaded.

Not much is left here of the 'satyr-play'. Gone are the 'seductive power', the 'comical and spine-chilling' effects, the 'nihilistic humour'. What was earlier a 'basically political intention' has become a 'political main motif', and the politics are explicitly those of the war. The antitheses are now personified in figures we recognize as Settembrini and Naphta, although these—far from dating back to before the war—owe their existence to the much more powerful controversies Mann has lived through since his earlier letter to Amann. The most substantial component of Settembrini is Heinrich Mann and his ideas, and the adjective 'unvirtuous', here ironically applied to Hans Castorp's sympathy with death, takes its meaning from those passages of the *Betrachtungen* which argue the shallowness of Heinrich's rationalist 'virtue'.

Nota bene, it is now explicitly Hans Castorp's sympathy with death, not just his author's. This much does appear to have been decided. From the almost neutral object of a sardonic joke, Hans Castorp has become a medium for the expression—albeit artistic rather than frankly polemical—of the work's inner tendency. His past contact with death has grown into his main positive quality. He has become much more his author's man.

Along with this growth in his significance, one can guess at a matching positive valuation of the sanatorium world. This too had acquired extra meanings from the clash of war ideologies and was not merely the

milieu in which 'interesting' abnormality could be developed in a mediocre youth. Its major features, disease and timelessness, were both apt
to express the positive terms which Thomas Mann opposed to Heinrich's
'virtue'. For how does he define that shallow quality? As

> the absolute and optimistic siding with development, progress, the times,
> 'Life'; it is the renunciation of all sympathy with death, which is negated
> and condemned as the ultimate vice, the extreme of spiritual rottenness.
> 'I have the gift of life', declares the author of that lyrical-political poem
> which has Emile Zola as its hero, 'for I have the deepest passion for
> life! . . .' On the basis of Reason, one is virtuous, one takes the oath of
> allegiance to Progress, one furthers like a stalwart opportunist the 'natural
> development of things', one denies thoroughly the sympathy with death
> which one is perhaps not unacquainted with by virtue of one's *origins*,
> and by doing all this one achieves, in case one should not have had it from
> the first, the gift of life . . .
>
> Without a doubt this is the art of becoming healthy again. But the
> problem of what 'health' means is not a simple one . . .

This onslaught on the *Zivilisationsliterat* makes plain who was
behind the 'advocate of "work and progress" ', the 'disciple of Carducci,
eloquent in the Latin manner'. The attack on Heinrich Mann for his
shoddy attempt to overcome decadence and nihilism can be read as an
account of the broadening conception of *Der Zauberberg*. The refusal to
take sides with 'the times' and their development implies the ideal of
rising above the times—an ideal which Thomas elaborated in his theory
of nonsocial art, the 'many-sided' artist, and true 'aestheticism'. What
better to stand for this detachment than the Mountain world, elevated
and abstracted from time? And if Heinrich, by denying his nation and
the brothers' common roots was taking an all-too-easy road to 'health',
then the subtler world of disease acquired a positive value. So the sanatorium, with its height above life and its plumbing of the depths of
disease, came to stand, in Mann's mind if not yet on paper, for the values
he had formulated in the *Betrachtungen*. The original sardonic story
provided him with the thematic basis. War and the *Betrachtungen* gave
the themes broader reference. And one other work had been a technical
preparation: *Königliche Hoheit* (*Royal Highness*), the first attempt at
allegory, at an 'intellectual work of art in which ideas could clearly show
through'.

Can we be sure that Mann was consciously forging the components
for an allegory? Suggestive is the way he now gives the phrase *Sympathie
mit dem Tode* a representative meaning. On the one hand, that original
chink in the armour of Hans Castorp's normality has now become his
prime quality; on the other, it has become Thomas Mann's catch-phrase

for all those deeper characteristics which distinguish Germans from their Western enemies and critics. Hans Castorp stands for these characteristics; and when personal and general are linked in this way, allegory is the result.

Especially revealing is the allegorical mode of a page from the *Betrachtungen* chapter on 'humanity'. Still intent on showing up the one-sided vision of life Heinrich expounded, Thomas Mann asked whether men's dignity lay wholly in Promethean gestures of emancipation, whether the attitude of reverence was not aesthetically more acceptable. He then gives an example:

> I need only look up from my desk in order to refresh my gaze with the vision of a moist grove through whose semi-darkness the architecture of a temple shimmers white. A flame burns on the sacrificial altar, its smoke is lost among the trees. Broad stones, set in the marshy flowered ground, lead to the altar's shallow steps, and there, solemnly humbling their humanity before the Holy, figures in priestly robes are kneeling, while others, erect, approach from the direction of the temple to perform the service. Anyone who saw in this picture by the Swiss artist, which I have long valued and felt an affinity with, an offence to human dignity, might be rightly called a philistine. Yet the political philanthropist is no doubt obliged to see it as just that—and so much may be admitted, that it offers only too striking an example of the unreliability of art as a means to progress, and of its treacherous proclivity to an anti-Reason which can create beauty. But obviously the humanity of emancipatory progress is either not the true or not the whole humanity . . .

The Thomas Mann of 1917—he finished this chapter late that summer—is using Arnold Böcklin's *Heiliger Hain* as an allegorical medium to express his own ideas. But surely not for the last time. A temple, a sacrificial stone, hints of a terrible ceremony, all indicating that there is a side to humanity which rationalism ignores—these will recur in Hans Castorp's vision in the snow, in that second scene within the temple. Its mood and its meaning are close to this *Betrachtungen* passage and clearly owe much to Böcklin, just as the summer scenes outside the temple derive much of their detail from paintings by Ludwig von Hofmann.

But the interesting thing is the difference of emphasis between the 'Schnee' vision and this forerunner. In the novel the dual nature of existence is again being presented in place of views which are 'either not the true or not the whole humanity'. But by this time, even if Settembrini's western rationalism is being corrected, so too is Naphta's extreme 'anti-Reason'—some of the detail for which comes verbatim from Thomas Mann's wartime arguments. As for Hans Castorp, he is more aware of the dangers of excessive 'sympathy with death' than of the need to integrate it into a mature view of life. His author has gone beyond one correction to another, larger one. Hans Castorp's declared preference for Settembrini over Naphta, contrary to the balance of power in their disputations, is a symptom of this new attitude. In other words, the central vision of the novel strives to restore balance in a different, very nearly opposite sense to the page of the *Betrachtungen* which anticipates it.

The reason is that by the 1920s Thomas Mann had changed his view of the themes his novel was committed to formulating. He himself had completed the education which *Der Zauberberg* relates. That is how the *Bildungsroman* became possible, and necessary. Beginnings of an education were of course implicit in those 'pedagogical intentions' he mentioned to Amann in 1915, and more strongly still in the personification of rival principles which the 1917 letter to Amann records. If Mann did not yet use the term *Bildungsroman*, it was probably because he could not yet connect the fundamentally serious project his novel was becoming with a genre he could only imagine treating as parody: he called *Felix Krull* a parody of the novel of education and personal development, as part of a concession that he had contributed to Germany's 'dissolution by westernizing intellect'. Nevertheless, the name matters less than the substance. What was lacking in the earlier stages to make the work truly a *Bildungsroman* was the element of error. As yet the issues were too clear-cut, Mann's assurance too great to achieve the half-rueful tone typical of the genre. The translation into art of his seemingly final *Betrachtungen* insights required nothing beyond the more direct and cocksure mode of allegory. But changing his mind meant changing his mode.

True, large elements of allegory remain in the finished novel. Settembrini's clothes for instance, old and worn yet carried with elegance, and Hans Castorp's nickname for him, Italian organ-grinder (always the same predictable old-fashioned tune) encode a judgement on his liberal-individualist views and their rhetorical delivery. When he switches on Hans Castorp's light, he is Enlightenment Man. More broadly, the sanatorium world itself has the meaning discussed above, although this will eventually appear in a critical light. Hans Castorp's vision in the snow, which contains what Mann called the 'result' of the novel, is an allegory within an allegory, and the expedition leading up to it recapitulates Hans Castorp's whole Mountain adventure to date, the influences he has undergone, and their result. In the closing pages of the novel, the moods of the Berghof inmates stand obtrusively for the moods of pre-war Europe, and the Naphta-Settembrini duel takes place in the spot where Hans Castorp had so often tried to think out the true yield of their endless word-battles.

But all these things are finally only means within a more complicated economy. Allegory does not learn as it progresses, it knows the answers from the start and they are relatively straightforward. But in *Der Zauberberg* the hero moves from being a normal young man, in whom bizarre experience then brings out qualities and interests undreamed of, back to being a normal young man again. His penchant for disease, which the story had to activate, has to be toned down again, offset, integrated. Hans Castorp's words to Clawdia on the two ways to life, one ordinary, direct, 'well behaved', the other bad, going via death, the way of genius, interpret positively a development which has turned back on itself. They subtly convert into spiritual progress what might seem simple regress.

This is the very essence of the *Bildungsroman*. The temptation to say that Hans Castorp's author marched him up to the top of the hill only to march him down again is checked when we remember that such a movement can be accommodated uniquely in this genre, where past error becomes gain and gives shape to the story of a life.

"Bildung" in *The Magic Mountain*

W. H. Bruford

Erich Heller writes of *The Magic Mountain*: 'I have heard critics say that it is too talkative a book and, like other books by Thomas Mann, too ostentatiously knowledgeable for a work of the imagination. This criticism misses the very point of the work, for it is knowledge that is the subject matter of the novel, and the mind that comes to know is its protagonist.' It would be equally true to say that in this novel, more obviously than in any other work of Thomas Mann's, though many of them show the same tendency, his principal theme is a typical modern man's search for 'Bildung', for the insight, the development of his innate faculties as well as the knowledge, which will make life seem meaningful even to-day. *The Magic Mountain*, more obviously than any other novel of this author, is in the tradition of the 'Bildungsroman'. As we read it, we are interested more in the development of its hero's attitude to life in general than in the young man himself, for he is intentionally made passive and colourless, but unusually eager for daily new encounters with men, knowledge and ideas, so that by reflection on this experience he may learn in due time how someone constituted as he is may make the best of life. *Buddenbrooks*, *Tonio Kröger*, the Joseph novels and *Dr Faustus* all reveal an author who is almost intimidatingly cultivated, and who assumes in his readers a similarly wide range of interest in civilized values and ideas, but *The Magic Mountain* is more instructive than any of these other works as a reflection of contemporary attitudes, German and European, as Thomas Mann saw them, in the period immediately preceding the First World War. The novel appeared in 1924, but it had been begun, as a *Novelle*, in 1912.

From *The German Tradition of Self-Cultivation: "Bildung" From Humboldt to Thomas Mann*. Copyright © 1975 by Cambridge University Press.

In *The Magic Mountain*, by exploiting the advantages opened up to him by his choice of a place for the action, a large international sanatorium in the Swiss Alps, Thomas Mann is able to parade a great variety of individual and social types before the eyes of his openminded and endlessly curious hero, without shifting him from one milieu to another in search of significant experience, as his predecessors in the Novel of Development had been in the habit of doing. This device provides the occasion for innumerable conversations between Hans Castorp and a whole series of colourful characters but, like the unity of place convention in classical drama, it confines the author within narrow limits in his invention of external happenings. It also makes necessary a patient and very self-centered hero. Clawdia Chauchat's remarks to Hans Castorp in their last conversation seem to suggest not only that he is to be taken as typically German, but that the passion for 'Bildung' of his fellow-countrymen has some dubious aspects for foreigners. She says:

> It is well-known that you [Germans] live for the sake of experience—and not 'for the sake of life' [like her friend Mynheer Peeperkorn]. Self-enrichment is what you are out for. C'est ça, you [yourself] do not seem to realize that that is revolting egoism, and that one day you [Germans] will be revealed as enemies of humanity.

This is an idea to which we must revert at the end of our inquiry. It suggests a possibly catastrophic result for the world of the German preoccupation with 'Bildung', if it remains self-regarding and 'uncommitted', causing the individual to neglect his social ties with his immediate environment and the wider world. The high-minded but disastrous indifference to politics which Thomas Mann was finally to condemn so strongly, after sharing it for over half of his life, is one aspect of this neglect.

To lend greater probability to Hans Castorp's openmindedness and thirst for experience, Thomas Mann makes him a Hamburger, a member of an old-established merchant family, who had lost both parents before he was seven and been brought up by a great-uncle, with all the comfort and attention due to a young patrician, certainly, but without a parent's love and guidance. At school too he had been vaguely aware of the lack of any firm convictions about the aim of life in his teachers, of their 'hollow silence' on such matters. As he grew up, he enjoyed as a matter of course the creature comforts of civilization expected by one of his class, and he accepted passively its one absolute principle, a quasi-religious respect for work, but even this was not with him an inner conviction and he easily found excuses, e.g. in his persistent anaemia, for not over-exerting himself in his studies, and for seeking exemption from military service. At the age of twenty-two, when he visits his consumptive cousin Joachim at the Berghof sanatorium, having been advised to take a holiday himself in good air after the unaccustomed strain of his engineering examinations, he still has a mind which is open and impressionable, whereas Joachim's is quite closed to anything not connected with the military career which is his single aim in life. He thinks it best not to have any personal opinions and simply to do one's service, to be in fact what Hans, adopting his friend Settembrini's interpretation of Joachim, calls a 'lanzknecht and purely formal existence'—a reminder that one function of Joachim in the novel is to represent the military outlook on life.

But Hans Castorp's thinking too is less free than he sometimes imagines. He remains the Hamburg patrician he is by birth and education, who already as a child had felt so deep a sympathy with his conservative grandfather. 'Children and grandchildren look at people, in order to admire', the author comments, 'and they admire in order to learn, and to develop the hereditary potentialities which lie within them.' Instinctively, at times of stress, he reverts to gestures and habits he had observed in his grandfather, especially his way of burying his chin in his cravat. An important consequence of his deeply rooted consciousness of his rank is that he remains entirely cut off from the life of three-quarters of his fellow-countrymen, the working and lower-middle class, and at the Berghof he meets hardly anyone except the comparatively well-to-do people who can afford its fees. Occasionally patients turn up whose behaviour arouses comment, like the affected Frau Stöhr, with her malapropisms and general stupidity, or Herr Magnus the brewer, a prosperous industrialist, content to see Germany made into one great barracks, as long as there is business efficiency and solid workmanship behind it, no matter if politeness be lacking. But in general we have the merest glimpses of industrial and commercial life, always from above, and we hear nothing at all about the landowning and farming classes, and the agricultural workers under them, nor about the millions of factory hands. Whole aspects of the nation's life, like party politics or the social movement are similarly hardly touched upon. So the well-known dictum of Georg Lukács, that Thomas Mann gives us a picture of the 'total social reality of the time' by bringing together in one place a 'representative cross-section of its society', must be taken with more than a grain of salt. Even *Wilhelm Meisters Lehrjahre* (*Wilhelm Meister's Apprenticeship*) gives us a fuller picture of the German life of its time.

What Thomas Mann does give us is a vivid picture of the Berghof, its landscape setting, its staff, organization, daily and seasonal routine, and above all its international clientèle as distinct individuals, afflicted in differing degrees with the same disease, and generating together a psychological and intellectual atmosphere quite unlike that of the world outside. The habitual reactions and values of the Berghof patients are as far removed from those of the good citizen of Hamburg as those of the bohemian crowd of actors in the *Lehrjahre* had been from Wilhelm's boyhood world, and the effect of his transplantation on the hero is very similar in some respects. It makes them both begin to doubt some of the assumptions implied in the middle-class code, especially concerning work and 'respectable' behaviour. Hans soon learns from Joachim that living up at the Berghof one changes, for example, one's ideas about time. Three weeks are like a day, and the normal feeling for time is soon lost. One comes to accept idleness too without a trace of bad conscience. Before long Hans realizes, first through his early meeting with the Half-lungs Club, that sickness and death are also not taken seriously, as in the plains, but easily become 'a sort of spree'. This self-protective mechanism of wretched creatures in dissolution is reinforced by the staff's way of handling the frequent casualties among the patients—their use of the safe interval while most patients are at meals for the administration of the last sacrament or the removal of coffins—and the doctor's angry reproaches to a young man who makes a fuss about dying.

Immediately after his encounter with the frivolous young pneumothorax patients, on his first morning walk with Joachim, Hans Castorp also meets Settembrini, the Italian humanist and arch-intellectual with an itch for pedagogy, and hears the first of many tirades against the insidious wiles of Hofrat Behrens, the doctor in charge of the sanatorium, a brilliant display of malicious criticism, 'the brightest weapon of reason against the powers of darkness and ugliness'. The frivolous patients and the shabby intellectual are equally remote from Hans Castorp's native bourgeois temper, and both serve as eye-openers for him, much as the actors and aristocrats had done for Wilhelm Meister. But the serious young engineer, though he soon comes to share the feeling prevailing at the Berghof of belonging to a group exempted by illness from taking thought for the future, and happily resigned to 'timelessness' and the suspension of responsibility, finds himself listening with ever growing interest to Settembrini's discourses and, not without occasional protests, lets the Italian make him the chief object of his pedagogic passion. It is Settembrini who first makes him aware of 'Geist', of all that the exercise of his inner freedom can mean for him, while confined by illness to the Berghof. It becomes his university, and his spirit blossoms here, as his intellectual interests are gradually aroused. Settembrini, the son of a scholar and poet, and himself a writer, is the spokesman of the Voltairian humanism of the Enlightenment, of mercilessly critical reason spiced with malice, detesting superstition, and therefore fiercely anti-clerical, but obstinately optimistic about human perfectibility.

Along with this new rational influence on his hero's 'Bildung', Thomas Mann introduces the irrational, 'Asiatic' attraction of the door-banging Clawdia Chauchat, with her contempt for convention, and also, for a time, the spectacle of Herr Albin's desperate jesting, as he plays ostentatiously with his knife and revolver, threatening at any moment, as one beyond recovery who can 'laugh at it all', to make his own quietus. Hans Castorp too has a vision of escaping from the 'pressure of honour', his respect for what people think about him, into the final freedom of nihilism. So the very correct and conventional upper middle-class Hamburger finds these two different forms of escape opened up to him in his early days at the Berghof, a one-sidedly rational and a one-sidedly irrational one, and for long he experiments with both. For the first time he realizes the inhumanity of his rich friends in Hamburg, seeing it, through Settembrini's eyes, as 'the natural cruelty of life', of 'nature' not yet humanized by 'culture'. But Settembrini mistrusts his rapid conversion, and ascribes these criticisms to the disturbing influence of the Berghof itself, where people 'easily get lost to life' and find a sort of new 'home'. He urges him to go back at once to Hamburg, to escape from this insidious atmosphere of irresponsibility. His place is with life, not death, and his romantic assumption that disease is allied with intelligence, with genius, and is more 'distinguished' than health, is a mere relic of medievalism. It is a perfectly natural, not an abnormal phenomenon, as Hans had been inclined to think, that a woman like Frau Stöhr can be both ill and stupid. Hans has come to the Berghof as one whom the shock of early bereavements, the death of his parents and grandfather in his early childhood, had made already 'vulnerable and sensitive . . . to the harsh and crude aspects of an unthinking worldly life, to its cynicism, we might say.' Thomas Mann suggests further that the mysterious attraction which the boy Pribislav Hippe ('Hippe' means 'scythe'—the scythe of Freund Hein, the figure of death in German popular mythology) had exercised over him at school, when he was only thirteen, had been in some way associated in his mind with his reverence for death. Mme Chauchat had immediately reminded him of this Slav boy with his high cheek-bones and Kirghiz eyes, and she came to be symbolic for him of all this irrational temptation to be 'half in love with easeful death', and to link the idea of love with that of disease, encouraged as such thoughts were by Dr. Krokowski's lectures on this subject.

Thomas Mann had used a figure with many of the characteristics of Settembrini already in the *Betrachtungen eines Unpolitischen*, written during the First World War, but there this 'Zivilisationsliterat' . . . had been presented as his own antipode, based on his brother Heinrich. Now Mann's hostility to this type of thinking has vanished, and Settembrini is evidently to be regarded as relatively justified. Joachim is made to apply to him a phrase very like that used, as we saw, by Carlyle's disciple John Sterling when trying to sum up the essential qualities of the Germans of Goethe's time. What Joachim says is that Settembrini 'thinks well of man in general'. For Settembrini, the humanist has taken over the role of the priest, but his reasonable moralism, unlike that of classical Weimar, is inescapably political. Patriotism means for him radicalism, the hatred of tyranny of a follower of Mazzini, whereas for Hans and Joachim it means conservatism, as it had for Mann himself in the *Betrachtungen*. Literature is for Settembrini utterly committed to the fight for progress, helped by the beneficent influence of technical advance in uniting the peoples of the earth. He belongs to the 'League for the Organization of Progress' and is engaged on the volume concerned with literature for a collective work on *The Sociology of Suffering*. His way of speaking about progress as the 'natural tendency' of mankind, a belief which for him Darwinism only reinforces, suggests to us the ideas of the eighteenth-century Freemasons, even before we learn from Naphta that Settembrini belongs to the brotherhood. The leading Masonic aim, according to Lessing's *Ernst und Falk*, had been to overcome current prejudices about creeds, nations and classes. Similarly Settembrini holds it to be a matter of individual conscience to fight for social reform, pacifism, popular education and all such liberal causes. It is not in self-development that he sees 'Bildung', but in self-dedication to the political liberation of oppressed nationalities and the improvement of the conditions of life for all on earth.

The first effect on Hans Castorp's conversations, on the one hand with Settembrini and on the other with Dr Behrens, who arouses his curiosity about the human skin and bio-chemistry, is to start him off on an ambitious course of scientific reading, when he has provided himself through a bookseller in the village with text-books on human anatomy, physiology, psychology and all the sciences bearing on life. After these he turns to physics, to find out particularly about atoms and molecules and the infinitely small, before going on to morbid anatomy, infectious tumours etc. All this is very different from the book on *Ocean Steamships* which he had brought with him to read on the journey. It represents part of an educational programme comparable with those we have found, for example, in Goethe and Stifter. Hans is still learning from Settembrini too, at Christmas, for instance, about the historical importance of Christianity in the evolution of his kind of individualistic democracy, through its doctrine of the value of each individual soul, and the brotherhood and equality of all men as God's children. But the novelty has worn off this teacher's discourses, and Hans has begun to see the limitations of his abstract rationalism. The death of a patient well known to him reminds him that the love of freedom, the human attitude singled out by Settembrini in his praise of all that man can achieve by his own effort, is only one of the two basic tendencies of human thought. The other, it seems to Hans, is piety, the awareness of death in its solemn power, and of human weakness and fragility. The humanists have no monopoly of moral dignity, as one might think from Settembrini's harangues. The truth is more complex:

> Everything is human[e]. The Spanish attitude, God-fearing, humbly solemn, observing strict limits, is a very estimable variety of humanity, it seems to me, and on the other hand one can cover up with the word 'human' any kind of slackness and slovenliness—

an observation with which Joachim, as a soldier, warmly agrees. Hans feels too that there are other forms of morality besides Settembrini's 'practical tasks in life', 'Sunday fêtes for progress' and 'systematic elimination of suffering'. He finds it intolerable to live, as they do at the Berghof, with people suffering and dying in neighbouring rooms, while they themselves act as if it were no concern of theirs, and allow the management to maintain the pretence by spiriting coffins away at mealtimes and so on. He persuades Joachim to join him in visiting the 'moribund' and taking them flowers. He does this not only from Christian pity, but also as a way of satisfying his need to take life and death seriously, in contrast to the many who stay on unnecessarily at the Berghof because they like its permissive atmosphere, but there is perhaps some irony here, because his own reason for staying is not always entirely above suspicion. Settembrini, hearing of these charitable works, pronounces him to be a 'worry-child of life', who himself needs to be cared for, though the author tells us later that the new preoccupation of his hero arose out of a spirit of 'Bildung' opposed to that which inspired Settembrini as a teacher. It seems very like what Goethe in the *Wanderjahre* had found to be specifically Christian, the 'reverence for what is below us', namely suffering, disease and everything repugnant to the living.

The other irrational influence, represented by Clawdia Chauchat, is allowed a climax, in which its nature is made more explicit than hitherto, before Clawdia disappears for a long time from the Berghof, just about half-way through the novel. The chapter 'Walpurgis night', with a title recalling the scene in *Faust, Part I*, of the witches' annual festival on the Brocken, from the text of which Settembrini quotes appropriate lines at intervals, describes the celebration of 'Fasching', Carnival, on Shrove Tuesday at the Berghof. As Clawdia passes by, in her new sleeveless gown of brown silk, Settembrini murmurs: 'Lilith is here', continuing, when Hans asks 'Who?' 'Adam's first wife. Look out for yourself!' 'This Lilith', he explains, 'became a phantom of the night, dangerous for young men through her beautiful hair.' He reproaches Hans for using the familiar 'Du' to him, even on this privileged night, because he is doing it 'only from the pleasure in licence'. But Hans goes on to justify himself at length, and to express in rather extravagant terms his gratitude to his mentor for the pedagogic interest he has taken, in the last seven months, in a 'worry-child of life'. Surprised at this outburst, Settembrini exclaims: 'That sounds like a farewell!' as indeed it proves, for Settembrini never again plays the prominent role he has had till now in Hans Castorp's education.

His protest about the use of 'Du' turns out to have been a hint in advance of the author's intention in making Hans use the same familiar form of address to Clawdia, against her wish too, in all their following conversation, which he initiates by asking her for a pencil, ostensibly for a parlour game that is being played. In reality he is consciously establishing a parallel between this love scene and his boyish infatuation with Pribislav Hippe in their school playground, where the borrowing of a pencil had already served as an excuse for his approach. In the dreamlike scene between Hans and Clawdia when, speaking French, which gives their encounter for him an air of irresponsibility, he forgets the German and bourgeois love of order which Clawdia half mocks in him, and as they watch the grotesque figures of the dancers in their fancy dress, urges her to accept his love, so long suppressed, there is a clear suggestion that he has reached another stage in his 'Bildung'. He is not the orderly Hamburger in this episode, but the adventurous son of the Hanse. That the love of adventure has its place in morality too is indicated in Clawdia's words about the conversations she has regularly in her rooms with a Russian friend. They talk about many things, even about morality.

Hans has been to some extent accustomed to dangerous thoughts like these by his reflections about Dr Krokowski's lectures. He claims now that it is his love for Clawdia which is the real source of his illness. It is a genuine passion worthy of these surroundings, 'de la folie, une chose insensée, défendue et une aventure dans le mal', and not simply 'une banalité agréable, bonne pour en faire de petites chansons paisibles dans les plaines'. His claim to a tragic passion hardly carries conviction, with Clawdia or with the reader. One feels it is one more 'experience' he is seeking. He concludes his strange suit with a page of poetico-physiological variations on the theme: 'Le corps, l'amour, la mort, ces trois ne font qu'un', thoughts about the mystery, the shame and the beauty of organic life, on its twin foundations of love and death. With ideas which remind us now of Novalis, now of Wagner, old Romantic doctrine reinterpreted in the light of Dr Krokowski's Freudian outpourings and the fruits of Hans Castorp's recent reading, he woos Clawdia 'd'une manière profonde, à l'allemande', to be rewarded by her reminder, as she leaves, to return the pencil. It is only later that we learn he did so, and received in return her X-ray photograph to carry in his pocketbook.

Still another phase of Hans Castorp's 'Bildung' opens in Book VI, after Clawdia's departure. His preoccupations are at first apparently more coolly intellectual than ever, the study of botany, astronomy and the early history of mankind, varied by private talks with Dr Krokowski about abnormal psychology. Soon the cousins find themselves listening again to Settembrini, now living not at the Berghof, but in modest lodgings in the village. But Settembrini no longer has everything his own way intellectually. Hans hears him only in his passionate arguments with the Jesuit Naphta, an adversary carefully contrived by Thomas Mann to represent the intellectual revolt against reason in contemporary Europe. If reason is to be shown as vulnerable, it must be seen to be secretly motivated by self-interest, or class-interest, and this is what Naphta repeatedly suggests. At the same time he cannot honestly claim to be disinterested himself. His point of view must be seen by the reader as substantially explained by his origin and history, and the intellectual contest between him and Settembrini becomes the expression of a clash of interests and wills in the pre-1914 world. In the first argument Naphta begins with a Marxistic criticism of Settembrini's humanism, asserting that it is essentially bourgeois self-interest rationalised, the philosophy natural to a commercial and industrial middle class, utilitarian rather than humane, and eager above all to justify the freedom of the individual to make his own fortune without interference from outside. True humanism, on the other hand, comes from the civilizing work of the Church and its moral discipline, and it can only be restored now in a hierarchic society by the alliance of throne and altar—an ominous phrase for liberal ears! Naphta sees no genuine idealism in the liberalism praised by Settembrini, who looks forward to a future Europa dominated by the peace-loving nations. What is really coming, Naphta says, is a fierce conflict of rival capitalistic nations. A catastrophe is inevitable, it is the fate that Europe has brought upon itself. Settembrini insists on the idea of peaceful progress, human perfectibility through reason, but Naphta sees the nations as confused in their aims, and asserts that war might be a remedy for many current ills. Listening to these arguments, Joachim, speaking of course as a soldier, but perhaps also as a more typical German than Hans, remains unshaken in his conviction that it is best for the private citizen to have no opinions, and simply to do his 'service' as ordered. Hans however is left with much food for solitary thought on the bench by the mountain torrent, where he spends hours trying to think things out about life and the world, or 'ruling' as he calls it.

When the cousins visit Naphta in his suprisingly well-furnished rooms over a tailor's shop, in the same house where Settembrini lives in a bare attic, the object which first arrests their attention is a fourteenth-century 'pietà', a crudely carved and painted statue of the mourning Virgin with the dead Christ across her knees. Naphta describes it as a Gothic work, in which everything expresses most forcibly suffering and the weakness of the flesh, yet in these repulsive features reveals spiritual beauty. What Settembrini criticizes, when he joins the party, is the admittedly intentional departure of the artist from truth to nature, and he proceeds to hold forth on the beauty of natural form, as the Ancients conceived it in classical art. To his surprise, Hans takes the other side, and the discussion continues between Settembrini and Naphta on the respective merits of form and naturalism in art, the latter being in Naphta's eyes a reflection of the degradation brought upon man by science. He believes its triumph to be a passing phase, which will be followed by a reaction lasting perhaps two or three hundred years, and culminating in a revival of scholasticism and of an earth-centred cosmogony, the medieval view of the world in all its glory. This sounds like Thomas Mann playing with Nietzsche's idea of the eternal recurrence. It can only happen, Settembrini replies, if we completely abandon our present conception of truth, and agree to accept as true what is good for us, which means, politically speaking, whatever the state requires. Naphta accepts this necessity, but with the important proviso that a distinction shall again be made as in the Middle Ages between a man's duty towards God and his duty towards the world. The state must acknowledge the Church as supreme. What exactly is meant by 'Church' comes out only gradually. Settembrini of course points out that what Naphta proposes will mean the end of individualism, of personality, human rights and freedom as now understood. Naphta retorts that they have almost gone already, and that what we need in their place is discipline from a new master, the deepest desire of the young at least being always to have someone to obey. The new authority can only be established by terror. He evades at first Settembrini's insistent questions about who is to impose this terror, asserting that men are ruled at present by money. Finally he prophesies that our present plutocratic system will be replaced by the dictatorship of the proletariat in the form of a Christian communism. That will go against the grain with intellectuals, but it will be carried through 'in the sign of the Cross', with the ultimate aim of winning universal recognition for the belief that all men are equal as God's children. The accompanying political ideal will be a classless society, in which the state will have withered away, the Marxist dream, instead of the liberal one of a capitalistic world republic.

Naphta is evidently invented as a mouthpiece for various anti-liberal strains of thought current in Europe round about 1914, and still more ten years later, which can be effectively brought into contrast with the ideas of the liberal intelligentsia. Settembrini, for all his one-sidedness, is a much more credible character. It is only when Hans Castorp has had a full dose of his teaching and learnt from it what he needs that Naphta is brought in, in the second half of the book, to redress the balance and make Hans more critical. He finds now that there are philosophies totally opposed to Settembrini's agnosticism and liberal individualism, his belief in democratic institutions and self-determination for all peoples, his humanitarian opposition to class and national wars, and so on. There are some obvious self-contradictions in Settembrini's doctrine, as the author evidently means us to see. He preaches pacifism, for instance, but would be ready at any time to fight in an Italian 'war of nationality and civilization' against Austria. He is altogether too didactic and too sure of himself for Hans Castorp's liking. For all his irony, he can never laugh at himself; we are told in fact that he never laughs at all. In this respect at least Naphta is more human, as he laughs heartily at some of Settembrini's ideas—but again, not at himself. In spite of Thomas Mann's ingenious story of his origins and upbringing, he remains a paper monster. He is supposed to associate piety with cruelty from his childhood memories of his father, the kosher butcher, so he defends the death penalty and confessional procedure—the attempt, in criminal cases, to extort a confession from the accused by hook or by crook. Like many famous Jews—one thinks first of Heine—he was by instinct a revolutionary, and at the same time something of an aristocrat, so when at the age of sixteen he was offered a Jesuit education, he readily took to it, especially as he soon came to think of the Catholic church too as both revolutionary— because it was unworldly and unmaterialistic—and also intellectually distinguished and elegant. His brilliant intelligence found satisfaction in the subtlety of his teachers, although their otherworldliness and Christian charity apparently left him unmoved. An orderly system of beliefs has become more important for him than morality, and he is enough of a Romantic to find the dignity of man in sickness rather than in health. Curiosity prompts him to look into the theory of communism, he finds in it the same systematic intellectualism, the same hardness and dogmatic 'certainty' as in Catholicism and he persuades himself that the two systems can be combined. What this means must be that he is fundamentally a nihilist, for the basic contradictions between them are surely irreconcilable. It is not surprising that Settembrini finds logic in Naphta only on the surface, and beneath it a hopeless confusion, an interpretation confirmed by Naphta's suicide.

By the time that Hans Castorp has been at the Berghof for a year, his attitude to the place has come to be very different from that of his cousin. Joachim by now has lost patience with the repeated postponements of his return to his unit, and insists on resuming his military career, against the advice of Dr Behrens. Hans, who is told he could safely leave, stays on, chiefly, as he admits to himself, in the hope that Clawdia will return. His relatives in Hamburg, hearing from Joachim of his unaccountable behaviour, send his uncle James to investigate matters, but uncle James himself nearly succumbs to the lure of the Berghof and beats a hasty retreat.

In the masterly chapter 'Snow' the author shows us his hero, after a narrow escape from death in a snowstorm, making up his mind on the ultimate questions. Thomas Mann explained his intentions in writing this chapter soon after the appearance of the novel, in a speech at Lübeck. He admits here that as a typical Lübecker, he is more interested in towns than in the countryside, but says there is one element in nature which has always fascinated him, the sea. 'The sea is not a landscape, it is something that brings us face to face with eternity, with nothingness and death, a metaphysical dream, and to stand in the thin air of the regions of eternal snow is a very similar experience.' His attitude to nature in this form he sees 'as fear, as a feeling of strangeness, of an unseemly and wild adventure', and he points to the expression of this feeling in the 'Snow' chapter of *The Magic Mountain*:

> Look at little Hans Castorp, as in his civilian breeches and on his *de luxe* skis he glides into the primeval stillness, the highly menacing and uncanny, the not even hostile, but sublimely and unrelatedly indifferent! He takes on the contest with it, as he naively does with the intellectual problems on heights his fate drives him to scale, but what is the feeling in his heart? Not a feeling for nature, if that implies any sense of belonging together. No, fear, awe if you like, religious dread, physical and metaphysical horror—and something else too: mockery, genuine irony facing the immensely stupid, a contemptuous shrug of the shoulders in front of gigantic powers, which in their blindness can indeed physically overwhelm him, but to which even in death he would offer human defiance.

In the chapter itself, it is hard to find anything resembling the defiance expressed in that last sentence, which reminds one of Bertrand

Russell's *The Free Man's Worship*. 'For the sake of kindness and love, man shall not allow death any control over his thoughts.' That is the sentence, emphasized by the use of letterspacing, the German equivalent of putting a word or passage in italics, with which Hans Castorp's description of his dream ends, the dream in which, sheltering from the storm and half stupefied with fatigue, and from the effects of an unwise swig of port from his pocket flask, he had had a vision which invites symbolic interpretation. Its first part had been rather like the vision of all possible human delights conjured up for Faust by Mephistopheles after their first meeting. In an idyllic sunny landscape,

> Men and women, children of the sun and sea, were everywhere moving about or resting, sensible, carefree, handsome young people, so pleasing to look upon—Hans Castorp's whole heart opened wide, painfully wide and lovingly at the sight of them.

But wandering among these happy people, his attention is directed by one of them to a sort of temple, in the depths of which he sees horrible witches, eating the flesh of a child. Such horrors lie in the human past and are still part of life, we are given to understand.

> The great soul, of which you are only a fragment, perhaps dreams at times through you, in your way, of things which she is always dreaming of in secret,—of her youth, her hopes, her happiness and peace . . . and her meal of blood.

After this experience Hans is able to put into words what he feels himself to have learnt from the interminable arguments of Settembrini and Naphta, from his experience with the living and the dying at the Berghof, and from his reading. As Thomas Mann says in the Lübeck speech, it is the old doctrine of the golden mean, seen now as the essence of the ethos of the German middle class. A few extracts from Hans Castorp's reflections may indicate their general drift, though the effect of the many echoes of his mentors' speeches will be lost:

> Were they so polite and charming to each other, the sun people, with tacit reference to this very horror? That would be a subtle and very gallant inference for them to make! I will take sides with them in spirit and not with Naphta—nor with Settembrini either for that matter, they both talk nonsense. The one is full of lust and spitefulness, and the other can only blow his little trumpet of reason and imagines he will bring even madmen to their sober senses, all nonsense, surely. It is philistinism and mere ethics, irreligious, so much is certain . . . Man is the master of opposites, they exist through him, and therefore he ranks higher than they do. Higher than death, too high for it—that is the freedom of his head. Higher than

life, too high for it—that is the piety in his heart . . . I will be good. I will allow death no control over my thoughts! For that is what charity and loving-kindness mean, and nothing else.

Next summer Joachim is back again and the discussions with Settembrini and Naphta are resumed, the first topic being Freemasonry, interpreted by Naphta as a terroristic movement, but by Settembrini, himself a Mason, as still profoundly humanitarian, but no longer unpolitical, as in the age of Lessing, its aim being the perfection of humanity through a world league of Masons. To Hans privately Naphta reveals that Settembrini, being poor, has had difficulty in becoming a Mason at all, because the fees are high, most Masons being men of substance. ' "Bildung" and money, there you have the bourgeois! There you have the foundations of the liberal world-republic.' Freemasonry, in a word, is 'the bourgeois rabble formed into a club'. In a later discussion with Naphta, Settembrini agrees that 'Bildung' is now a middle-class affair, but it is founded on the tradition of humane learning coming down from the classics. Literary genius is the noblest expression of the human spirit, and the man of letters, through his cultivation of the divine gift of language, is the modern saint. According to Naphta, this is sheer conservatism, clinging to a tradition which is not for all time, but simply the expression of the bourgeois-liberal epoch. German schools are already out of touch with reality and their pupils learn what is most valuable for them out of school through public lectures, exhibitions, the cinema and so on. Classical education is already despised by the masses as the ideology of the middle classes, and its days are numbered, a matter of decades at most. The final achievement of the liberal bourgeois has been pure nihilism, the destruction of all positive beliefs. These discussions link up, it will be seen, with what we have found in Nietzsche and Fontane, who would presumably have sided with Naphta and Settembrini respectively.

The seventh and last chapter introduces a new figure, completely unlike any of the types of suffering, pleasure-loving or thinking humanity we have encountered at the Berghof so far. It is the Dutch coffee-planter Mynheer Peeperkorn, an outsize old man with a shock of white hair, eccentric in speech and habits, clearly used to command, but no intellectual. Settembrini finds him just a stupid old man, but for Hans Castorp he is strangely impressive. 'He could put us all in his pocket', he says, because Peeperkorn makes him realize that there is a mysterious, positive value in sheer personality. He is one of the men of passion spoken of by Clawdia in the passage quoted early in this essay, who live for the sake of living, and not just to extend the range of their conscious experience. This 'self-forgetfulness' is something foreign to Hans Castorp's nature, but as a born 'culture-traveller' (an ironical description, of course, on the analogy of 'commercial traveller') he has the panoramic ability, to use a phrase early applied to Goethe, to appreciate and get to like even one so diametrically opposed to himself. He sees that Peeperkorn 'has a thing about being able to feel, a sort of *point d'honneur* about being fully alive', as he explains to Settembrini, who feels however that there is a good deal of self-dramatization about it, and that Hans is 'venerating a mask'. Peeperkorn is certainly full of mannerisms, some of them, as Mann admitted, copied from Gerhart Hauptmann, like perhaps his habit of raising his eyebrows, and thus furrowing his forehead horizontally, to make his small eyes look bigger. Anyhow, Hans and the planter take to each other, although they are rivals for Clawdia's love. She has felt pity, she explains to the sympathetic Hans, for Peeperkorn's 'anxiety about feeling', the sentiment that drives him to suicide after taking part in a final excursion to a splendid waterfall, symbolic of the dynamism which he worships and feels himself to have lost. After exposing his hero to torrents of words about life and its problems, Thomas Mann apparently felt it necessary to bring in this odd character to remind Hans, not without his usual irony, of what Goethe called 'the incommensurable', the inexplicable quality of life.

The remainder of the last chapter, after the death of Peeperkorn, shows us a Berghof overshadowed by the approach of the First World War, the state of Europe being reflected in that of the collecton of sick Europeans at the sanatorium. Hans finds all around him the evidence of stagnating life—the section is headed 'The great stupor'—a stagnation which people try to forget in bursts of meaningless activity, in hobbies like photography, stamp-collecting, puzzle-solving, in learning Esperanto or merely playing patience. We are reminded of the political events leading up to the War by an occasional remark, e.g. by Settembrini's mention to Hans of the threat to Austria implied in current Russian diplomacy, a warning which Hans, though full of forebodings, is at the moment too deep in a game of patience to heed. Then for a time Hans is quite absorbed in the newly discovered delights of music, the Berghof having acquired a good gramophone, which Hans operates, often for hours alone. We hear much about his favourite records, all highly characteristic, 'Der Lindenbaum', for instance, with its Romantic association of love with death, 'you would find rest there'. Even a craze for spiritualism develops from which Hans, still a 'culture-traveller', does not hold himself aloof, till he is shocked to the point of revulsion by the calling up of the spirit of Joachim, who had died soon after his second return to the army. Finally 'The great exasperation' sets in, a time of senseless impatience and quarrelsomeness among the Berghof patients, shared of course by Settembrini and Naphta, both now seriously ill, and no longer disposed to take each other's sallies with good humour. A reference to the *Titanic* disaster fixes the time as the spring of 1912. Naphta becomes more and more bitter in his ridicule of Settembrini's ideas:

> The world republic, that would be happiness at last, surely! Progress? Alas, he was reminded of the famous sick man, always changing his position in the hope of relief. The unacknowledged but in secret quite general wish for war was an expression of this. It would come, this war, and that was good, although it would have different results form what those planning it promised themselves. Naphta despised the bourgeois safety-state . . . War, war! He had no objections, and the general lust for it seemed to him comparatively creditable.

What finally drives Settembrini to exasperation is a harangue by Naphta, at coffee in a Kurhaus, on an excursion the pair make with Hans and two others in winter, a monologue on the problem of freedom, full of irony about the 'deeds' committed in its name. Indignant at the 'infamous' ambiguities which his pupil Hans is being compelled to hear, Settembrini calls on Naphta to stop, and a quarrel ensues which leads to a duel. Settembrini's justification of a final appeal to force in a private dispute is at the same time an explanation of the inevitability of war in the Europe of 1914:

> The duel, my friend, is not just an institution like any other. It is the ultimate, the return to the primeval state of nature, only slightly moderated by certain conventions of a chivalrous kind, which are very superficial. The essential about the situation remains the absolutely primitive corporeal conflict, and it is every man's business, however far from the natural his life may be, to keep himself prepared for this situation.

At the duel Settembrini fires into the air and Naphta shoots himself.

Not very long after the duel, while Settembrini is still alive, the War breaks out, and this at last drives Hans Castorp, after seven years at the Berghof, back to the plains. Our last glimpse of him is in battle, and it is left an open question whether he will survive, for the novel, we learn at the end, has been 'A hermetic story', told for its own sake, not for his. 'Hermetic' refers back to Naphta's description of the initiation ceremony of the Freemasons in chapter VI, where Hans had been told that the neophyte 'must be eager for knowledge and fearless', that the grave was the chief symbol of the initiation, and that the way of purification led the young man eager for the wonders of life through the fear of death and the realm of decay, clearly a parallel to Hans Castorp's quest for 'Bildung' at the Berghof. Now at the end of the long process Hans is called 'an uncomplicated young man', well fitted for his role because of an adventurous strain in his character inherited from his Hanseatic forbears. In the Lübeck speech Thomas Mann gives us a good brief reminder of his new novel's main theme, when he speaks of his hero's 'Hanseatic nature',

> which proves itself not after the manner of his forefathers in superior piracy, but in a quieter and more intellectual way: in his enjoyment of adventures of the heart and mind, which carry this ordinary young man off to the realm of the cosmic and metaphysical, and make him truly the hero of a story which undertakes, in a strange and almost parodistic manner, to renew the old German Wilhelm-Meister-type 'Bildungsroman', this product of our great middle-class epoch.

The traditional Bildungsroman, as the product of a stable society, had usually shown how the initially callow but openminded and lively hero had after varied experiences and innumerable discussions with people of all kinds found his feet in the world. Like most novels for the general reader, it ended happily and with the implication that with the lessons he had learnt, the hero was ready for whatever the future might bring. *The Magic Mountain* can be said 'almost to parody' this kind of novel in that the hero comes to terms, in the course of it, not so much with life as with death, or at least with death as the ever-present shadow of life. Already as a boy Hans feels a certain fascination for the phenomenon of death, and in seven years at the Berghof he lives surrounded by the suffering and the dying and, though he feels the lure of the irresponsible and learns through his two mentors how far along the road to nihilism the modern world has moved, he retains his generous humanity even when faced with the worst. A return to a happy life 'in the plains' was however an artistically impossible ending to his search, one ruled out anyhow by the explosive state of the world. It seems fitting that Mann should break away from the old pattern, and leave his hero facing with fortitude the hideous results of Europe's return to 'the ultimate, the primeval state of nature'. His long and complex mental development as an individual has brought him round to acknowledging the claims on him of the society into which he was born, though no doubt also 'with genuine irony facing the immensely stupid'.

The Magic Mountain

Henry Hatfield

It has been said that *The Magic Mountain* is comparable to no other novel, but one can hardly wish to forego all comparisons between Mann's novel and others. Indeed, since the book itself is a magic mountain on which it is easy to go astray, some sort of map is called for. Classifying the novel is pedantic only when it involves pigeonholing; a great work often belongs simultaneously to several categories at once. On this point the English scholar T. J. Reed writes cogently that *The Magic Mountain* "is spiritual autobiography, confession and apologia, an intricate allegory, a kind of historical novel, an analysis of Man and a declaration of principle for practical humanism."

Reed adds that it seems to parody the *Bildungsroman* but is really a serious example of the genre. Normally the *Bildungsroman* traces the development of a youth up to the point when he has achieved a degree of maturity and is ready to play his part in the world. Financial and social success is a very minor matter; renunciation is a frequent theme. On the other hand, a genuine novel of this type will show both intellectual growth and formation of character. Whereas the *Bildungsroman*—Goethe's *Wilhelm Meisters Lehrjahre* (*Wilhelm Meister's Apprenticeship*) is the great model—is the representative type of German novel, it is often formally deficient, unduly long, and meandering.

To be sure, fighting in a war whose causes he largely does not understand is not a very glorious end to Hans's education, but thus he is sharing the fate of a whole European generation. On the other hand, he has sensed, however vaguely, the humanistic significance of his vision in the snow. It is he who brings the rather nasty séance to an end, and he who tries manfully to prevent the bizarre duel between Naphta and

Settembrini. That he is able, by conscious willing or otherwise, to push aside the residue of his disease and serve in the front line is evidence that he has become an effective human being, almost over night.

From another point of view, *The Magic Mountain* may be seen as a "time novel" (*Zeitroman*), in three senses. It can be seen as a portrait of prewar European society during the period 1907–1914. Further, in certain sections—which are not digressions by any means—the novel directly discusses the circular nature of time, subjective versus objective time, and the polar relation between time and eternity. Finally, one can venture the supposition that the effects brought about by time in this novel render time an active force, almost a character.

A mighty, even a mythical, hero may be a rogue, and so can the protagonist of an educational novel; *Joseph and His Brothers* is an excellent example. Hans Castorp has a touch of rascality, as when he throws his mentors' pet phrases back at them. Yet despite Settembrini's repeated words to Castorp, "Engineer, you are a rogue," Castorp is really a very serious young man; and despite much humor and some touches of parody, the book is in the last analysis a very serious one. The theme of education, which superseded the original plan of a grotesque novella, also kept the many comic elements in a subordinate position.

Approaching *The Magic Mountain* in terms of experiment, adventure, and dream is a refreshing tactic. It makes Hans Castorp seem more active and more attractive than most interpreters do; there is more to his life than "soup everlasting" and peripatetic seminars. Although "placet experiri" (we are pleased to make experiments) was not Petrarch's motto as the novel implies it was, it definitely is Castorp's. Ludwig Völker gives a longish list of his experiments large and small, which cannot be rigidly separated from his adventures; the near-fatal foray on skis, for instance, is both experimental and venturesome. Castorp's most significant dreams afford insights which may lead to further adventures. Thus a dream of his boyhood friend Pribislav Hippe intensifies his fascination for Clavdia Chauchat. Whereas Castorp soon forgets his dream vision in the subchapter "Snow," the reader and the author remember.

As conceived and developed by Helmut Koopmann, in connection with Mann's work, the "intellectual novel" is not as radically different from the novel of adventure as it sounds. For the adventures on the mountain are predominantly intellectual, and the intellectuals are adventurous indeed in their theoretical constructions. Who but an adventurer, one might say a charlatan, would calmly "demonstrate" the near identity of Hegelianism and Catholicism, as Naphta did in his youth? In the realm of theorizing about intellectual matters, almost anything "went" in the Central Europe of those days. The narrator, however, is at pains to point out, when necessary, that the arguments of Naphta and Settembrini have become far-fetched, confused and confusing.

In moving toward a definition of the intellectual novel, Koopmann states that the top, realistic stratum of such a book is only a facade, and the reader who can realize this is superior to any "simple" hero. A strong tendency to "essayism"—comments by the author within the work on the book itself or related matters—is characteristic of such novels.

This view has its points but does not touch the heart of the matter. In a true intellectual novel, it would seem, the ideas must be more important than anything else; in *The Magic Mountain* they are significant but the human factor is central. Aldous Huxley, Musil, and Broch are genuine intellectual novelists in that they put ideas first. Koopmann's term does not imply praise or blame: Hesse's *Steppenwolf* appears as an interesting, though hardly great, novel of ideas. For all its wealth of historical discussion, *War and Peace* is more successful with people than with ideas.

Possibly "novel of intellectual adventure" is a more useful label for *The Magic Mountain*. For while Hans Castorp has adventures of several kinds—medical, erotic, and outdoor—it is clearly the intellectual which prevail. Generally, he tends toward experimentation and scientific curiosity; Mann even stated: "He thinks to experiment is truly to serve. He does not resist evil." In the midst of his most perilous venture, in the snowstorm, he recalls getting lost in the midst of the debates between Naphta and Settembrini. Certainly "intellect" plus "adventure" is a useful formula for making a good *Bildungsroman*. Yet there exist renowned novels of education, like Stifter's *Indian Summer*, in which there are no real adventures, spiritual or material. (There are experiences, which is a very different matter.) Hofmannsthal was one of the first to sense the live, endangered quality in Mann's novel, which is in many ways a static book. "What is primarily admirable, it seems to me, [is] . . . the courage with which the 'I' in this book leans far out over the abyss, over chaos, and without getting dizzy."

In the best sense, Castorp possesses Nietzsche's double perspective. Conservative yet daring, he accepts the traditional *Respice finem* (Think of the end) but corrects it with the Goethean "Remember to live." Settembrini's quoting of *Placet experiri* is repeated during the novel; the motto of the Hanseatic League, though not mentioned, seems equally relevant: "It is necessary to sail forth, it is not necessary to live." This statement is more typical of the Hanseatic spirit than the possibly frivolous *Placet experiri*. It does not hold life lightly but implies that there are values still more important. When the narrator, here surely identical with Mann, remarks at the end of the novel that it is not a matter of great concern whether Hans lives or dies, the statement does not reflect indifference or diminish the stature of the hero in any way. Hans has broken the spell, has acted on his own, has saved his soul, even though history has forced life's problem child into the ranks of death.

If, as we are repeatedly told, Hans is a simple young man, how can he be "life's problem child" and the central figure of a novel of 1,000 pages? There are several answers. From his first conversations with his cousin Joachim Ziemssen one can infer that at times he is not simple at all. (Mann, who identified himself at times with Castorp, must have seemed simple to the teachers at the Lübeck Preparatory School who persisted in flunking him.) Further, there is no doubt that Hans Castorp matures as time goes on; he is "heightened" in the hermetic atmosphere of the sanatorium. Although his education does not proceed without setbacks and an unhappy period of stagnation, he finally emerges as a victor, even though he seems doomed.

His illness may well be marginal and psychogenetic; from Mann's point of view it is also a sign that he is not basically simple. Hans dimly senses that he should follow "the way of genius," which is dangerous and often evil, or at least not respectable. In his case this means leaving the solid satisfactions of a prosperous Hamburg burgher and withdrawing into a life that is mainly one of contemplation—for seven years. Without his illness, this change would have been impossible. Illness brings him freedom—as it brings freedom to his beloved Clavdia Chauchat. Another of the "advantages of shame" is that Hans is now definitely out of competition and all its worries. To realize that his light case of tuberculosis was at least partially a blessing in his own eyes, one need not consult Freud; common sense will suffice.

It should at once be added that Hans Castorp's fundamental experiences predispose him to passivity, illness, and a veritable cult of death. These experiences include continuity (traditional mores, family ties), death, freedom (from responsibility), love, as manifested in his adolescent devotion to Pribislav Hippe, and finally the conviction that contemporary society afforded no goals attractive to a thoughtful person. Indeed, there has been such an accumulation of deaths among the Castorps that one is reminded of the Buddenbrooks at the end of the family's career; Hans, however, is far less unstable than young Hanno. Nevertheless, Hans is convinced that death is more dignified and more noble than life, and illness is more conducive to profundity and genius than is health. Not entirely false, these views were inherited by Mann from various German romanticists, especially Novalis. It took Mann, like Hans, a long time to relativize them; he never completely repudiated them. Amusingly enough, Hans never thought it possible to be both sick and stupid until he encountered that dreadful Mrs. Malaprop, Frau Stöhr, at Berghof Sanatorium.

If Castorp is to be "heightened," he must have some inner substance from the beginning on which the alchemic processes can work. "Nothing can come of nothing." He has a good, if unspectacular, mind; he develops a keen interest in ideas and in various biological sciences. He is stimulated not only by his mentors and his love for Clavdia; presumably his tuberculosis has a heightening effect, as Leverkühn's syphilis does in *Doctor Faustus.* On quite a different plane, Hans is a kind and friendly person. One needs only to think of the various calls he and his cousin Joachim make on the hopeless cases, the *moribundi*. Perhaps the visits are made in part because of Hans's fascination with death, but that is not the whole story; it seems rather that truly felt knowledge of death makes a person more humane.

One crucial experience Hans had on the mountain is that "he looked into his own grave." The verb "see" with variations appears again and again in this passage. Seeing the bones of his hands under x-rays, he realized for the first time that he would die. Perceiving Joachim's lungs, even his heart, had been uncanny enough; but to see himself as a skeleton surrounded by far from solid flesh truly shook him. Thus it is not death or dying as such that educated Hans—these were everyday occurrences on the mountain—but the sudden, existential conviction of his own mortality. If it is true that many persons, perhaps most, never really confront the fact that they will die, then Hans has indeed had an educational and salutary shock.

Among other things, Hans Castorp's relationship with Clavdia Chauchat introduces or reintroduces him to love; his youthful love for Hippe had been hardly more than a crush. This love is frankly physical; in the seven months of waiting, before he has really spoken to Clavdia, he envisions life itself in the image of her naked body. She is the white-armed, slant-eyed, reddish-haired temptress, a Lilith or a Slavic Venus, to risk an oxymoron. (White arms occur often in Mann, always linked to feminine attractiveness.) To her, the standards of the flat land do not apply. For the rather passive, conventional Castorp to have won her, even for a night, was rather a triumph. As part of his emancipation from the burgher class, Hans comes to find it a good thing that the word "love" can cover both the most sublimated and the earthiest sorts of passion. His losing Clavdia to the aging but magnetic and wealthy Peeperkorn is presumably a part of his education, as is certainly his profound friendship with his cousin Joachim.

Anticipated by his vision of Hippe, the section "Snow" is the high point of Hans's development and of the novel as a whole. In the former section, he ventures rashly, not yet acclimatized, on a walk in the mountains, alone. Suddenly a violent nosebleed strikes him; he must lie down, and falls asleep. He dreams of Hippe, who had eyes apparently slanted, like Clavdia's, and of the same color. He recalls borrowing a mechanical pencil of a type we shall encounter again. Obviously, his unconscious is trying to tell him something.

Similarly, in "Snow," Castorp acts adventurously, even rashly. He goes out into the mountains on skis, and soon loses his way in the snowy wilderness. Caught in a sudden storm, he soon falls asleep in the snow. (The two antithetical, yet complementary, dreams he has during his brief sleep are central to the novel.)

In a long, impressive chapter of his book on *The Magic Mountain*, Hermann Weigand discusses the question "What is German?" Now there can be no doubt that one of Castorp's functions, in Mann's intention, is to represent the relatively stolid, solid, silent, musical German caught between Latin rhetoric and Slavic fanaticism. (Since it is very strange to call the Germans silent, Mann may be thinking that his nation did not make a good verbal case for itself in World War I.) As a citizen of upper-class Hamburg, however, Castorp would seem on the whole closer to an upper-class Britisher than to a Prussian lieutenant or a Bavarian peasant. Further, the quiet, contemplative type whom Castorp represents had been on the defensive since about 1870 and is very far from the bustling, pushy *arrivistes* so frequent in the empire of Wilhelm II, from the Kaiser himself down. Castorp is a German possibility, hardly the representative German.

In Joachim Ziemssen's case, we must ask a very different question. Why is he repeatedly called "the best of all of us up here"? Mann himself states that Joachim is much the less interesting of the two. It is obvious that Joachim accepts the mores of the German Army unquestioningly, and believes that serving in its ranks is the highest human bliss. In Settembrini's words, his is a "purely formal existence." Yet he combines a high sense of duty with a quiet, self-effacing manner; he seems to be *sans peur et sans reproche*. Apparently he refrains from making love to Marusja not out of puritanism but because he refuses to let anything interfere with the cure and his return to the Army, toward which he resolutely strives. He provides a base line, a norm, with which the other characters can be contrasted, whether they are bizarre sports like Naphta, Peeperkorn, and Krokowski or pleasure-seeking nonentities like most of the minor figures. Unlike these persons, Joachim is neither an intellectual, a pseudo intellectual, nor a nonentity. His death is one of the genuinely moving incidents in a book that tends deliberately to avoid any emotion which has not been x-rayed.

Why, we must next ask, is Mme Chauchat unflatteringly called the "hot cat"? Let no one think that Mann hit upon that name coincidentally;

Mann's universe is as controlled as Newton's. Since Mann was notoriously an admirer of canines (see *A Man and His Dog*, 1918), the name he chose betrays a certain distance from the lady, though hardly hostility to her. For one thing, Clavdia moves like a cat: she slinks (*schleicht*) rather than walks. To be sure, she can be most charming, but she seems to be essentially aloof. "But still I am the Cat who walks by himself," as the feline puts it in Kipling's story. If we may believe the hints of Behrens, La Chauchat is reasonably promiscuous in a feline way: attractive to many males, faithful to none. Clavdia's love of showing off in presenting herself to the other patients is also catlike.

Mme Chauchat is after all the representative of the East, as seen by many Westerners. How feline she is appears in the fact that she does not write even one line to Castorp during her absence from Davos. Toward Peeperkorn, she is relatively decent; but one has the feeling that if Hans talked the sort of nonsense Peeperkorn does and were equally wealthy, she might have been faithful to him—for a season.

Clavdia hates Settembrini, the champion of Western democracy—and of universal rules, norms, and decencies. Quite obviously, the narrator regards the Italian with affection, even though his intellectual model, the "civilization journalist" appears in the "Reflections" as the shallowest of men. The shift reflects not only Mann's reconciliation with his brother Heinrich (no longer called a journalist) but also his general acceptance of the postwar world, dominated as it was by the victors of 1918. Naturally this included the support, even the militant defense, of the Weimar Republic.

Despite his absurdities, Settembrini is vindicated as a decent, well-meaning man, not as a guide to the future. Anyone who speaks of "dedicating the burgher's pike on the altar" or compares the effect of the three days of the July Revolution to that of the six days of creation can hardly be taken seriously. From a Western point of view, Settembrini's flaw lies not in his liberalism but in his crucial failure to realize the great difficulty of reconciling liberalism with the nation-state. He warns against the dangers of totalitarianism, as we would call it today, but ignores those of capitalism; his antagonist Naphta takes the opposite position. While aware that the tyranny of the Romanovs is worse than that of the Habsburgs, the flaming patriot Settembrini holds that "Vienna must be hit over the head," so that Italy may make good its claim to the Irredenta. Generally, his causes are harmless if a bit ridiculous, like his Freemasonry and his participation in framing an "encyclopedia for the elimination of human suffering." Yet he is capable of making witty, penetrating observations: of Naphta he remarks, "His form is logic but his essence is confusion"; of the psychoanalyst Krokowski, "He has only one thought and that's a dirty one." Although he champions a militant foreign policy for Italy, he refuses to kill, and his farewell to Castorp, a potential enemy, could not be warmer: he kisses him on both cheeks and calls him "Du," for the first time in seven years. Still a very sick man, he returns to the Italian flat lands to work in the name of *sacro egoismo* for Italian entry into the war. It is virtually certain that neither he nor Hans will survive.

To understand Leo Naphta, one must try to see how the pieces of this human puzzle fit together—this Jesuit, Marxist, terrorist, and Jew. Of course he is a very unsatisfactory Jesuit, Marxist, and Jew. The first three categories suggest varying degrees of dictatorship and violence—though in the case of the Jesuits, the violence no doubt is or has become metaphorical. What Naphta calls *Kultur* is the existence of a high intellectual and aesthetic world in an atmosphere dominated by dictatorship and violence. Spain in the sixteenth century or the Middle Ages as seen by Naphta himself would be excellent examples; if Vergil or Horace had flourished under Caligula, Naphta would be vindicated. Further examples of his ideal are the cannibalistic second part of Castorp's vision in the snow, or the expressionists' notion of Gothic man. It seems right that a man of Naphta's acuity and learning be Jewish; also a remarkable number of Jewish intellectuals have become Marxist—among them Georg Lukács, now identified beyond doubt as the model for Naphta. Sharpness of mind, argument, and profile are characteristic of both. Of course there are important differences between the real Lukács and his *Doppelgänger*. Thus Lukács was not a medievalizer, nor (so far as known) addicted to secret luxuries. Sharp though he is, Naphta could hardly have coined Lukács' aphorism: "Talent is always a rightist deviation." Naphta is subtly allied to Clavdia Chauchat: both reject the normal, the rational, and the moral (as morality was envisaged in middle-class European society around 1900).

Naphta commits suicide; in retrospect it seems inevitable. First there was his traumatic boyhood experience of seeing his delicate, intelligent father crucified in a pogrom by enraged peasants, presumably Russian. This atrocity must have marked him permanently. (Mann wrote of him as a "desperately brilliant reactionary.") Since he finds killing the highest joy, he is desperate indeed. Jesuit though he is, he barely mentions Jesus; in fact, he is so devoid of love that he cannot even love himself. When he calls Settembrini a coward for refusing to shoot at him and shoots himself, he reveals the psyche of a desperado: when he stated that capitalist society willed its end he may well have been right, but he was projecting his own death wish upon it. That he kills himself in the bizarre duel with Settembrini suggests that those who build on hatred will destroy themselves.

Like Leo Naphta, Pieter Peeperkorn is both a synthetic character, drawing on Nature figures like Dionysus and Tolstoy, and a biographical one, modeled on Gerhart Hauptmann. Until the Nazi period, the most prestigious twentieth-century German dramatist (most of his better work was done before World War I), winner of the Nobel Prize in 1912, Hauptmann was called by Mann "King of the Republic" in the Weimar years. At the same time Hauptmann had ridiculous aspects, liking to pose as the older Goethe, whom he vaguely resembled, and to make all sorts of solemn pronouncements which often did not mean very much. In his drinking habits he too was an authentic Dionysian, and in his very ambiguity he was the type to appeal to Mann: like his image Peeperkorn, he was a "blurred personality."

As a "chunk of Nature"—Mann believed that Nature is in itself inadequate—Peeperkorn is Naphta's opposite. Peeperkorn cannot finish an articulate sentence except on such a bizarre topic as the properties of various poisons. Yet he has a truly charismatic personality. With apparent ease, he annexes the unpredictable Clavdia. Clearly, she does not sell herself for money alone, but *pecunia non olet*: money is not offensive to her nostrils. The kitten wants her cream. None of the masculine characters even makes a strong attempt to stand up to Peeperkorn. As discarded lovers, Hans and Hofrat Behrens simply have to put a good face on things. Naphta and Settembrini are swept aside: the Dutchman is no intellectual and often not too intelligent, but when he dismisses their debates as "cerebrum, cerebral" or speaks half articulately about "the sacrament of lust," no one else is listened to. Instinctively, Peeperkorn identifies himself with natural forces: thus he urges an eagle, soaring far above him, to strike and kill. Like the eagle, he too is "royal." (Mann had been impressed by the anecdote that the old Tolstoy sympathized with a hawk which threatened to attack his chickens.) For Peeperkorn, the one disgrace, the only sin, is impotence. He envisions life as a naked woman, spreading her limbs before the man and challenging him. Similarly, Castorp had pictured life in Clavdia's image. The earthy Dutchman even uses the term "our mistress" for her.

Clearly, Peeperkorn is intended to play the role of a twentieth-century Dionysus, and as long as his body permits, he does just that. It has been pointed out that Mann drew on Hauptmann's *Heretic of Soana* (1918) for the pagan side of Peeperkorn's creed. Not only does he drink on a heroic (or an insane) scale; not only is sex his favorite theme; when drunk, he makes advances to all the women in sight, including a dwarf. The orgy in the section "Vingt et Un" repeats and varies Mann's "Walpurgis-Night," at the same time marking the high point of Peeperkorn's re-enactment of Dionysus. Very soon the frame of the myth changes: the millionaire decides to give a feast, and soon an ill-assorted group has assembled for a quasi Last Supper. Apparently no Judas is present; they are only twelve in all. When his guests succumb to sleep and wine,

Peeperkorn identifies himself with Jesus. "Wine—," he said, "women;
they are—that is—pardon me—Gethsemane—Day of Judgment." On the
last day of his life, Peeperkorn "is" the Man of Sorrows and a pagan priest
almost simultaneously. The waterfall by which he poses drowns out the
sound of his voice; probably this is symbolic of the impotence he fears
so profoundly. That his cult of sex is valid only up to the onset of old
age is obvious. Further, one should note the contrast between his role as
Dionysus, for which he seems well fitted, and his posing as Jesus, for
which he has no visible qualifications. Or should one ally Bacchic routs
with the bread and wine of Christianity, the Virgin Mary with Clavdia
Chauchat?

Edhin Krokowski, the somewhat unorthodox psychoanalyst, is an
even more dubious phenomenon. At the time that Mann was writing
The Magic Mountain he seems to have seriously read very little if anything of Freud, but Freud was very much in the air, as Zola had been
when Mann was writing *Buddenbrooks*. Any influence would have been
atmospheric, not specific. A few years later, Mann was to become perhaps
Freud's most effective lay champion, but at this point he generally dis-
liked what he knew or guessed about psychoanalysis. He had not yet
realized the centrality in Freud's thought of "where Id was, shall Ego be."

Mann allies the movement at this point with the dark side of German romanticism, particularly with the considerable part of Novalis'
ideas that is focused on sex. Further, the name Krokowski suggests the
Slavic East, hence, at least according to Western prejudice, a general
tendency to a lack of clarity and form. Krokowski, who wears a black
suit or overall and whose cellar office is two steps below Behrens', is
clearly a death figure. His tasteless dress, which combines a frock coat
with sandals, is even more repulsive to the relatively elegant Hamburgers
than is his symbolic role. He appears to be one of the tribe of faith healers
and gurus which flourished in Germany before and after World War I.
His facile use of the word "comrade" points in the same direction.
Whereas Krokowski seems to be the only figure in the novel to whom
Mann is unfair, he too teaches Hans a valuable lesson: that love is mul-
tivalent, not to be pigeonholed as physical, spiritual, or anything else.
When he states that all sickness is transformed love, he seems to have
stood Freud on his head. Although he appears to be rather a deluded
deluder than a charlatan, the narrator's hostility is obvious:

> Truly, he stood there, behind his little table, with arms outstretched and
> head bent to one side, and looked, despite his frock coat, like the Lord
> Jesus on the Cross.
>   It turned out that Dr. Krokowski, at the end of his lecture, was
> making grand-style propaganda for the dissection of souls, and with arms

outspread summoned everyone to come unto him. Come unto me, he said, though in other words, ye who are weary and heavy-laden. And he left no doubt as to his conviction that all, without exception, were weary and heavy-laden.

True to the dogma of *Placet experiri*, Hans has some analytic hours with Krokowski, but these sessions seem to be neither frequent nor significant. Probably Krokowski provides a modish side attraction for bored patients. For his part, Hans so desperately desires Clavdia that no mere words, not even hers, can really help him.

In the second half of the book, Krokowski focuses his interests more on the "occult" and less on analysis. Doubtless Mann, in the early twenties, thought less of the latter and more of the former than most people do today; he granted some truth to each but had very grave reservations about both. His essay "Experiences of the Occult" tells of attending a séance in Munich, presided over by a Baron Schrenck-Notzing. The whole performance he found sordid and degrading; but to put it bluntly, the novelist was taken in. In *The Magic Mountain* he uses the words "murky nothingnesses" to describe the contents of the occult occasion, yet after experimenting like his spiritual offspring, Mann was convinced that the manifestations he observed were genuine.

Castorp can hardly be faulted for taking part in the same adventures as the author. When Hans was outraged by the performance—which seemed to bring the dead Joachim back to life—he suddenly put a stop to the whole event, gaining greatly in stature. Repeating an earlier gesture of Settembrini's, he turns on the light. This is a long step toward the ideals of the People of the Sun and toward life. As for Krokowski, he is not a bad fellow but seems hopelessly involved with the forces of night.

A curious expression occurs often enough in Krokowski's realm of death to be worth noting. Just before Joachim Ziemssen dies, he moves his right hand "with a scraping, raking movement, as if he were gathering something in." Similarly, in "Experiences in the Occult," the medium makes "scraping movements" of his hand and arm before returning to the ordinary world. Finally, Elly Brand, the medium in *The Magic Mountain*, acts "as if she were gathering something and drawing it in." This gesture, it appears, accompanies the passage from life to death, or vice versa, either in reality or in the course of a séance. Birth and death appear as reciprocals.

Whereas Krokowski is known as the Rat Catcher (the Pied Piper in the English version), Hofrat Behrens is the Bird Catcher, from *The Magic Flute*. From Goethe down to Hesse, Mann himself, and Auden, Mozart's opera has been the delight of civilized men. In contrast, the Rat Catcher is clearly sinister; with some shock we recall that Krokowski is a cellar-dweller, as are the rats. In other words, however artful Behrens may be as the Bird Catcher Papageno, he is colorful and amusing. No one can accuse Krokowski of possessing these qualities.

With the exception of Peeperkorn, the director of the sanatorium, Hofrat Behrens, is the most ambiguous figure in a novel that teems with enigmatic persons. Most of these have a basic "set" or tendency of character: who would deny that Naphta is evil, Settembrini good or at least well-meaning, Clavdia feline? In Behrens' case, however, his ethics as a doctor and the state of his health, among other things, are dubious. We see him acting his role very ably, but we hear from Settembrini quite damning things about his policy in running the Berghof. Quite possibly the rhetorical Italian is exaggerating. Yet Behrens does seem at times unduly sensitive about his honor. In the section, "Choler, and Worse" (translated also as "Fury and Another Painful Matter"), Castorp tactlessly questions the doctor's decision to let him return to the flat lands. Behrens puts the worst possible construction on his words, as if Hans were blatantly questioning his integrity; he shouts, quite gratuitously, that he is not operating a bawdy house nor is he a pimp, though Hans's wish to stay on at the Berghof is simply a matter of waiting for Clavdia.

One fact is fundamental: Behrens does not own the Berghof but is the medical manager for the consortium which does. To keep in the good graces of these invisible rulers, he must show profits consistently; this in turn might well influence him to behave unethically. Clearly, Behrens' lightning diagnosis of Hans smacks of proselytizing. (Mann had experienced this sort of recruitment when he visited his wife in Davos.) On the other hand, there is no hint that the financial state of the Berghof would call for such cheap maneuvers; quite the contrary. And if Hans is not very sick, neither is he very well. In this case, no line can be drawn between ethical and unethical, and the verdict on Behrens must be of the Scotch type: "Not proven." He is capable of great decency, as becomes evident in his treatment of Joachim, his mother, and Hans, during the last days of the soldier's life.

Another very deep split in Behrens' character and role lies in the personal realm. Continually he cracks jokes, usually in student slang, yet underneath he is a sad person, subject to recurrent fits of melancholy. In part he plays the fool to amuse his patients, but the reader feels that this comic mask is one Behrens must wear, willy-nilly. Quite aside from that, he can be spontaneously witty. When Hans Castorp, speaking of a coffee mill with lewd ornaments, ventures the banality that the ancients more or less equated the obscene with the holy, the Hofrat remarks, in an offhand manner, that the donor was "more for the former, I think."

His sexual life is also subject to severe tensions. Apparently, sex is very much on his mind, as becomes clear in various conversations and in his "in-depth" portrait of Clavdia, who has almost certainly been his mistress. None of this seems to bring him lasting satisfaction.

An aspect of Behrens' career takes us back to one of Mann's earliest obsessions: the physician is an artist, a sick artist, and there is a causal relationship between sickness and art. He is a dilettante with the brush, but his portrait of Clavdia convinces in its very sensuality, whereas the paintings of an idealistic Behrens woud be failures. One need only think of Tonio Kröger's damning remarks on amateur writers with lofty intentions or of Felix Krull, a success *because* he was a crook.

Whether Mann consciously planned it or not, that it is the artist or semi-artist Behrens who instructs Hans Castorp on the question of form is not insignificant. "Form" is used here, in the section "Humaniora," in the broadest sense. In their discussion, Castorp is well on his way toward sweeping aside the differences between life and death; he is in his *enfant terrible* mood. Behrens checks him: "Life means that during the changes of matter, form is preserved." With sophomoric persistence, Hans asks "Why preserve the form?" and later rises to the remark: "Form is lah-dee-dah." Like other good sophomores, he outgrows before long his barbaric adolescent attitudes. This brief passage is crucial for if "form" is accepted as important, we are really in a *Bildungsroman* situation. Further, there are strong links between "form" and the "People of the Sun" envisioned in the section "Snow." Perhaps to imply that "form" is not merely a matter for aesthetes, Mann has a physician who is only marginally an artist explain and vindicate it.

The brief but important preface should be mentioned. Mann calls it *Vorsatz*, which more often means "intention" or "introductory phrase" (in music), but here also means "preface," beginning his novel with a triple pun. In a page and a half, he makes several important points: Castorp is a "simple" fellow, but is not wholly so; his story took place long ago (that is, before World War I), which is seen as a major turning point in human history; the narrator will tell his story in detail, believing that "only the thorough is truly entertaining." Heaven forbid that the task will take him seven years! Partly by indirection, he informs us that the nature of his hero is complicated; that there is a musical element in the work; that time will play a significant part. Even the narrator's perhaps half-serious fascination with the number seven is briefly apparent. As so often in music, several of the book's notable themes are sounded at the very beginning.

There are in *The Magic Mountain* certain particularly impressive scenes, or set pieces. The x-ray scene and the dream of young Hippe are two of them; the vivid depiction of the carnival brings the first half of the book to a climax, *fortissimo*. By entitling the section "Walpurgis-Night," Mann is to some extent risking comparison with one of the most effective scenes in Goethe's *Faust*, which depicts a great gathering of witches and their male colleagues and is also set on an enchanted mountain. A rash venture, one would think, but Mann has shifted his focus to the passion of Hans and Clavdia. In *Faust*, whether or not the reader literally believes in witches, the element of evil is very real; on Mann's mountain, people on the whole are pathetic rather than wicked. Clavdia Chauchat and Frau Stöhr correspond to the Young and Old Witches who dance with Faust and Mephistopheles, respectively. Goethe writes of his young, handsome witches as naked; one could argue that the x-ray photo of Clavdia is still more so, but it is hardly erotic, except perhaps to necrophiliacs.

The opening of Mann's version is parodistic in a light, even gay fashion. Versed in Goethe as in the Italian poets, Settembrini quotes the "Walpurgis-Night" repeatedly. To him, a carnival enacted by the sick and the dying is a mockery, but his sarcastic quotations are generally taken as sheer fun by the other patients. When Hans Castorp, rather drunk, defies the Italian and partially emancipates himself from his pedagogic influence, we have the first serious element of the scene. Hans's education, or better initiation, makes real progress. On a reduced scale, he re-enacts the role of

> The priest who slew the slayer,
> And shall himself be slain.

While Settembrini remains Hans's friend and *one* of his teachers, he loses any semblance of power over him. His stupid attempt to keep Castorp away from Mme Chauchat ensures his defeat. Calling her a Lilith figure, a witch, is no way to destroy the spell she has cast over the young man; quite the contrary.

Since it is the night of the carnival, Hans can finally address Clavdia with the informal "Du"; he could not bear to use the formal term. After seven months of slow pursuit, Hans has ventured an approach; he may prevail, like the tortoise in Aesop. When he speaks to Clavdia, he is deathly pale; perhaps it is fear of rejection which has so quickly sobered him. Borrowing her pencil, he is keenly aware of the parallel to the pencil Hippe once lent him, long ago. Eternal return! His telling Clavdia that his fever was caused by love for her is a signal that he is still "half in love with easeful Death," an engineer obsessed with the ideas of Keats and Novalis, though probably he has never read either one.

His brief but most intense love affair with Clavdia constitutes the second and more important initiation he undergoes on the fateful night of the carnival. (His youthful visit to a brothel is rather a commercial transaction than a true initiation.) If it seems surprising that she accepts him, after seven months of his apparent neglect, one must remember that she is radically unconventional, in part because her illness and her husband have set her free. (Hans is so much impressed by her "Russian" view of life that he again rejects any notion of form; this relapse is not permanent.) More important, doubtless, is that she and Hans both espouse the same romantic ethos: true morality lies in sin, in abandoning oneself to danger. A final reason: she feels real, if limited, affection for this "joli bourgeois." A more complicated question is: why does Castorp suddenly take to conversing in French, evincing a most surprising control of anatomical terms? Partly it is because talking French, using an alien idiom, is like talking in a dream, as Hans puts it. The chief reason is less obvious: Hans's eloquent evocation of the female body—a seduction in words—is based on Walt Whitman's "I sing the body electric," in the translation of Mann's close friend Hans Reisiger. The well-bred Hans would not speak to a woman in German (or in English, the second language of many educated North Germans) about *les mamelons fleurissants* or *le sexe obscur entre les cuisses*. French, traditionally the erotic language, was the appropriate medium. By no means shocked, Clavdia soon responds to his unexpected directness. They become lovers almost at once, but Mann was not writing an erotic novel; she is dispatched the next day to a distant province of Russia.

Like "Walpurgis-Night," the section "Snow" is one of the highest peaks of the book. It starts rather negatively: masses of snow fall, and there is little sun, the patients complain. Yet the wintry landscape is a challenge to Mann's descriptive powers: he writes of "the gloomy nothing, the world packed in grayish-white cotton wool," of "white darkness," of "the white, whirling nothing." "Snow" and "white" are major leitmotifs; this choice of images seems obvious, but the result is not. Even more important is the repeated use of the word "nothing" or "nothingness" (*das Nichts*). Obviously it is related to the wintry landscape in which nothing grows and to the snowstorm which prevents all meaningful seeing. Above all it suggests the harshness of authentic, nonromanticized death and the nihilism to which Castorp almost succumbs. That he somehow snatches his vision out of "the jaws of death" is no accident; it is central to the entire novel.

Not wishing to be snowed in, Hans buys a pair of skis surreptitiously, athletics being forbidden to the patients. It is a long step forward from passivity to an afternoon's skiing in unknown, dangerous mountain country, where a snowstorm may strike at any moment. Settembrini, who encouraged Hans on these escapades, calls him Mercury, the god with wingéd shoes, but urges him to be careful. That Settembrini and Castorp are closely allied here foreshadows the eventual defeat of Naphta.

An adroit use of parallels heightens the effect of the scene. Noting the snowscape around him, Hans recalls walking along the shores of the North Sea during a storm. Once he had bathed in the breakers off the island of Sylt; a lifeguard (clearly a predecessor of Settembrini) had blown his horn as a warning. Such warnings Hans will ignore, but he has become very fond of the Italian, windbag though he calls him. When snow flurries obscure the contours of the mountains, Hans quotes a line picked up from Naphta: "Praeterit figura huius mundi" (The shape of this world passeth away). There is the sudden chill of death. As he had got lost in the endless debates between Settembrini and Naphta, he is now lost in the storm. Worse, as before he had rashly defied the breakers, he has now purposely lost his way in defiance of the Alpine world. We remember that he wanted to become ill long before.

Nowhere else is Castorp so close to the epic or mythic hero. And as will become clear, he passes rapidly from an extreme of danger to a maximum of insight. It is a situation best described by Goethe's "Stirb und werde" (Die and be reborn).

As the blizzard becomes blinding, Castorp gets seriously lost. He involuntarily makes a circle from and back to a small hay shed; this provokes his grim pun on *umkommen*, to circle or (normally) to perish. The workings of his increasingly bewildered mind are masterfully narrated: his thoughts are generally relevant but do not hang together; he is still astute enough to cling to the shed wall rather than to sink into the snow. Falling asleep, he has a dream which epitomizes the whole Germanic "drive toward the South" and especially the evocations of Italy and Greece from Winckelmann and Goethe to twentieth-century poets like Stefan George. The "People of the Sun," probably ancient Greeks, act with grace and dignity, with "noble simplicity and quiet grandeur." Statuesque, beautiful, and relaxed (Mann followed certain pictures by Ludwig von Hofmann in his descriptions), they seem the perfect examples of the classical life; they are representatives of Nietzsche's "Apollonian" Greeks. Still more they remind one of Goethe's Greeks, for they behave with a humane kindness not at all reminiscent of the authentic Hellenes. Even Hans "recognizes" them; he has seen them before. We think of Settembrini and his influence.

This perception is "corrected" only too soon. Hans is suddenly aware of a frightening archaic Doric temple: we have moved some centuries back toward barbarism. In the temple, two witchlike women are devouring a child. Behind Settembrini's world lies Naphta's; behind high classicism, far behind, lies cannibalism.

Not without some reason, it has been charged that the language of Mann's dream passages is overstylized, even precious. Outside of one or two sentences, I do not find it so; in any case, it should be remembered that everything is filtered through the quite unliterary consciousness of Hans Castorp. Further, Ludwig von Hofmann's Art Nouveau pictures seem to have influenced Mann's depiction, especially "The Fountain" (*Die Quelle*), which was hung in Mann's study. That Castorp should forget his graphic, memorable visions within a few hours has naturally been a stumbling block for many readers. But does he forget completely, or only with his conscious mind? Surely, something remains. His courageous and often astute actions described in the sections "Highly Questionable," "*Hysterica Passio*," and "The Thunderbolt" show that life's problem child is about ready for graduation. When he switches on the light at the macabre séance, Settembrini has won another symbolic victory. Despite all delays and relapses, Hans is moving from passivity to action, from shapelessness to form.

In "*Hysterica Passio*" (perhaps more accurately translated as "The Height of Wrath"), Mann uses his familiar technique of starting at a point of low tension and "heightening" the situation continually until the end of a story or chapter is reached. The first instance occurs when a young patient has paroxysms of irritability because his tea is cold. Far more serious is the case of the anti-Semitic patient, a very sick man. "Yet he was not a Jew, and that was the positive thing about him." Often fallible in political matters, Mann could be a sensitive political prophet, not only here but in his observation that the totalitarian Naphta, in these oppressive days, often crossed the border dividing intellectual health from insanity. As comic relief, the elaborate quarrels and ear-boxings among a group of punctilious Poles might have been excellent, except that the sense of impending storm makes it very difficult to find anything funny.

All this is but prelude to the bitter quarrel between Naphta and Settembrini, which makes their earlier skirmishes seem rather trivial. With his mocking words about freedom and its heroes, Naphta drives Settembrini to violent protest. He in turn uses words like obscenities, equivocations, and above all *infamy*—an indirect echo of Mann's reaction to his brother Heinrich's attacks on him during World War I. (Apparently, Heinrich's remarks were not meant as personally as Thomas believed.) Like the protagonists, the three bystanders sense that the only possible outcome of such a clash is a duel. They hear Naphta grind his teeth and invoke holy terror; Settembrini suddenly utters the words "mad dog." When Hans makes his first attempt to stop the insane conflict, Settembrini's words seem logical, but he has been psychologically manipulated into a warlike attitude by Naphta, whose terms for the duel are downright murderous. Hans's second try at making peace is equally frustrated. Naphta openly upholds bloodshed and war; maddened by Settembrini's shooting into the air (a sign of futility), he kills himself. Under the circumstances, his act is far the worse; this is not a case of "an antique Roman" falling on his sword, but of fierce hatred turning upon itself. As Settembrini is undoubtedly a representative of the Entente *Weltanschauung*, one might infer from Naphta's actions that the Jesuit was the appropriate spokesman for the Central Powers. Needless to say, that was not Mann's view. If Naphta represents any specific nation, it is probably Bolshevist Russia.

After the tension of the duel scene, the last section, "The Thunderbolt," opens with deceptive calm. People grow up, even in a sanatorium; others die. Toward the end of his seven years, Hans is virtually ignored by the physicians; as he was during the time when he failed a class at school. Again he lives through the primal experience of negative freedom. Utterly disengaged, one might almost say psychologically dead, he corresponds with no one and has even replaced his beloved cigar, whom he had spoken of as a girl friend, "Maria" and "she," with a Swiss brand. Worst of all, when his watch broke, he did not bother to have it repaired. No longer a citizen of the Western world, he might have sat by the Ganges with Siddhartha, or better, have joined the other shades in Hades. Already he has been relegated to the Bad Russian Table, the least prestigious of the seven.

When the thunderclap resounds, Hans is shocked out of his lethargy and rushes down to the flat lands to enlist. Yet he does not grasp at first just what is happening and why. He is "like a man . . . who has neglected to read the papers"—in other words, like the Thomas Mann of 1914. Realizing that he has not broken the magic spell or freed himself by his own powers, Castorp is grateful to life for liberating him, even for death. Recalling Joachim, whom he does not mention, he ventures to believe that over his own grave three salvoes will be fired. His illness has completely vanished, probably from his body, certainly from his consciousness.

Critics have argued that sending the young man off to a Belgian battlefield to die is a strange triumph for life; indeed it is. Nor are Hans's actions the result of a reasoned choice: he is no Hercules at the Crossroads, deciding calmly between good and evil.

Rather, as Settembrini says, he will fight bravely on the side to which his blood binds him. The Italian will fight on the opposite side, with the weapons of his rhetoric. That precisely the liberal humanist upholds the war and puts national, in part subliminal, values first is significant. What Mann implies is that in the mood of July and August 1914 almost everyone in the countries directly involved reacted more or less the way Hans did. The central paradox of the novel arises from the fact that its intellectual thrust is toward life, its historical thrust toward war. By no means a confusion, this dissonance comes from the contradictions of an era that produced Wilhelm II and Stresemann, Poincaré and Briand, in quick succession. Mann is tentative and cautious in appraising the situation. Envisioning the European battlefield, the narrator asks, in the last sentence of the novel: from this universal slaughter, shall not love rise up some day? This question may be cold comfort, a weak solution, to some, but this is an infinitely more responsible reaction to the situation than a grandiloquent slogan like "the war to end war."

The last scene, showing "three thousand feverish boys"—Castorp is one of them—as they try to charge through a concentrated barrage, is the most excruciating in the book. The tone is unsparingly realistic but not sensational; there is no trace of hatred toward the enemy, who is barely mentioned. The narration is uncomplicated, but with an important exception. As the attacking force rushes into an ever more desperate situation, Hans sings "The Linden Tree" to himself, unaware of just what he is doing. We recall from the subchapter "Fullness of Harmony" that this lovely lied expresses a longing for death; its text bears this out. Perhaps the song had a different burden a century ago, but now, in a new context, death is lurking behind Schubert's music. And yet, the man who died for the "magic song," that symbol of an earlier Germany, dying with the new word of love on his lips, was actually dying for the future, to overcome the magic song. This interpretation may sound egregiously dialectical but it means that the man who dies for the older, romantic Germany is also clearing the way for the new. *"Se non è vero, è ben trovato."* If one compares this passage with parts of Mann's address on Nietzsche in 1924, it is evident that "the new word of love" is Nietzsche's message that men, to overcome romanticism, must be true to themselves and to life. Various parallels, including a reference to the "magic song" of death, make this evident.

Mann has again shown how form can vanquish content. This novel of disease and death is far from morbid; this compendium of strange ideas is anything but intellectually misleading. To change to the point of view of a professional writer and quote Wassermann: "Landscape, atmosphere, narration, tempo: incomparable."

Nietzsche in *The Magic Mountain*

Alexander Nehamas

Aspects of Nietzsche's thought and imagery have not been difficult to locate in Thomas Mann's *The Magic Mountain*. We know that Hans Castorp's vision of the beautiful classical youths whose eyes acknowledge the reality of the horrible sacrifice occurring nearby owes much to *The Birth of Tragedy*. And while Mynheer Peeperkorn is something of a Dionysian figure, Naphta's Jesuitism is tainted with some of the master morality's coarser features. However, Nietzsche's influence has mostly been found only within such specific contexts in the novel and not in its more general or structural features.

This is due partly to Mann's claim that during the First World War he liberated himself from the exclusive influence of the late German Romantics, among whom he counted Nietzsche, and partly to the suspiciousness with which Nietzsche came to be almost universally regarded after the Second World War. Mann's intellectual development, following his own account of it, has been plotted against a continually widening horizon, from the more narrowly German to the more broadly European. Mann seems to have begun writing under Nietzsche's spell, but to have cast that spell away with the works of his maturity, of which *The Magic Mountain* is the first.

The interpretation of the way in which the characters are related to one another and to Hans Castorp in particular has been conditioned by Mann's working description of the novel as a "pedagogic story" in which Hans is placed between Settembrini and Naphta, the former standing for humanism, rationality, and progress, the latter for mysticism, unreason, and reaction. By focusing on *two* characters fighting over Hans, this description invites us to think that all the main characters are related

From *Philosophy and Literature* 5, no. 1 (Spring 1981). Copyright © 1981 by The University of Michigan - Dearborn.

to each other in such opposing pairs. And by picking out *these* two characters, it invites us to subordinate the others to them, and to consider the pedagogues' views as themes on which the others' are variations.

This thematic and structural dualism has determined the reading of *The Magic Mountain*. The novel's criticism has tended to see Castorp as beset by two antithetical but self-sufficient attitudes toward life: one can either celebrate it, if somewhat superficially, with Settembrini and his allies, or one can hold it in contempt, if quite morbidly, with Naphta and his camp. Hans is offered a choice between West and East, classicism and romanticism, democracy and despotism. He must side either with idea or will, either with reason or instinct. In the end, of course, Hans refuses both sides and so distinguishes himself from his companions. But his course is plotted between these two poles, to which all other ideas and characters in the novel are subordinated. But the characters are less clear and more equivocal, more "enigmatic," than they at first appear to be. Such ambiguities in motivation and thought are most obvious in the characterization of Settembrini, to which we now turn. For it is in the reasons for these ambiguities that we shall find the real influence of Nietzsche on *The Magic Mountain*.

"The fundamental faith of metaphysicians," wrote Nietzsche, "is the faith in opposite values. It has not even occurred to the most cautious among them that one might have a doubt here." Settembrini is just such a metaphysician: "Two principles, according to the Settembrinian cosmogony, were in perpetual conflict for possession of the world: force and justice, tyranny and freedom, superstition and knowledge; the law of permanence and the law of change . . ." Despite Naphta's quip, "Doesn't your monism rather bore you?", Settembrini's dualism is everywhere apparent. He is always pitting Reason against Instinct, Mind against Body, Spirit against Nature, Work against Lethargy, Europe against Asia, the Enlightenment against the Middle Ages. Where does this dualism originate?

Settembrini's grandfather was a political agitator, a *carbonaro* actively dedicated to the liberation of Italy. His father was a classical scholar who did not take to the streets but who broadened his concerns to the unification of Europe and "the attainment of general felicity." Settembrini turned his own attention to the nature and improvement of humanity itself, translating his political opposition to Austria into a metaphysical aversion for instinct in general. But, as Nietzsche remarks, "one should not try to exceed one's father's industriousness; that makes one sick." And so, the scion of a line of gradually widening concern and decreasing efficacy, Lodovico Settembrini ends up, like so many people he detests, ill on the magic mountain.

Indeed, he claims to detest the coarse, idle, vulgar, pleasure-seeking patients of the Berghof. To show his distance from them he even pretends not to remember the name of Frau Stöhr, whom he nonetheless knows well and with whom he flirts quite obviously in the dining room. And is not even his distaste a pretense as well? For in this environment, where acquaintances are not easy to make, Settembrini, "despite his contemptuous attitude toward the society of the place . . . always knew everything that went on." He is a source of medical histories, sexual escapades, social mishaps—despite his distance, the sanatorium's gossip.

Certainly, he disapproves of the moral laxness of the Berghof, and takes it upon himself to protect Hans from Clawdia's pernicious influence. But he belies his superior attitude by his adolescent behavior. He ogles and whistles at a village girl and pinches the cheek of one of the waitresses. He impresses Naphta with his petty vulgarity: "I did not know, Lodovico, that you were a prude. To see you looking at the girls . . ." And he never, it seems, goes farther than such gestures; his sexuality, like his practical efficacy, is stunted: "Ah, this Settembrini— it was not for nothing he was a man of letters, grandson of a politician and son of a humanist! He had lofty ideas about emancipation and criticism—and chirruped at the girls in the street."

And his illness, which Settembrini so detests, and which confines him to a life of inaction—how serious is it? How ill is the pedagogue? "Not dangerously, so far as I know," claims Joachim, "but obstinate, keeps coming back." He himself says that he is "unfortunately rather ill"; he does not follow his own advice to Hans to leave the Berghof immediately because, he asserts brusquely, his own case is "rather worse" than the engineer's. But there is little evidence for this, and Hans seems quite aware that Settembrini is unwilling to apply to himself the standard he expects his disciple to follow.

Hans, in any case, does eventually return to the world below, whereas Settembrini never ventures to the flat-land despite his express desire to do so. In contrast to Castorp's, his own work, he claims, "is at least of a nature that will permit me to carry it on, if needs must, even in this accursed place. . . . You are differently situated from myself, in that you can only pursue it down in the world . . ." His rationalizing of his withdrawal from that world is nowhere more apparent than in his explanation of why he never attended the meeting of the "League for the Organization of Progress": "I wanted to go—good God, I yearned to be there and take part in the deliberations! But that scurvy rascal of a Hofrat forbade me on pain of death, so—well I was afraid I should die, and I didn't go. I was in despair, as you may imagine, over the trick my unreliable health had played me. Nothing is more painful than to be prevented by our physical, our animal nature from being of service to reason." In this instance Settembrini gives his cowardice a metaphysical justification. And this justification is provided by a dualism of mind and body on which he insists despite Hans's objections: "my spirit protested in pride and anguish against the dictates of my wretched body."

Settembrini's metaphysical dualism may thus originate in an effort to account for his behaving in ways quite inconsistent with his avowed principles—in particular, for his choosing a life of inaction when all his values condemn it. But his very metaphysics is as inconsistent as his behavior. In the very same speech he claims to honor and love the body, yet continues to say that "within the antithesis of body and mind, the body is the evil, the devilish principle, for the body is nature." He even praises Plotinus for having "made the remark that he was ashamed to have a body." Yet later on, when Naphta accepts a view very like this, Settembrini has no difficulty in protesting vehemently against it. And when Hans Castorp repeats his remark on Plotinus, the humanist simply bullies him into dropping the subject: he "flung up his hands and ordered the young man not to confuse two different points of view—and for the rest to be advised and maintain an attitude of receptivity."

Settembrini's inconsistency is nowhere more apparent than in his social and political views. Though a pacifist, as he often says, he has no qualms in rising to Naphta's fateful challenge to a duel: "Theoretically, I disapprove of the duel, I am of a law-abiding temper. In practice, however, it is another matter. There are situations where—quarrels that— in short, I am at this man's service." The breakdown between Settembrini's theory and his practice is here reflected in the breakdown of his carefully controlled style. In his inarticulateness, moreover, he adopts the mode of speaking of Peeperkorn, the anti-intellectual worshipper of feeling he has already described as "a stupid old man," even to the point of using one of his favorite expressions, "in short." Faced with the inadequacy of his own theory, Settembrini is forced to borrow his values, and therefore his language, from Peeperkorn, and declares that, "however civilized," he is ready for the physical struggle. But when the time comes, by a second reversal which casts doubt on the strength of his resolution without convincing of the depth of his civilization, he proves unable to shoot his opponent.

Settembrini is a pacifist on the political level as well, and believes in a united democratic Europe. But both Hans and Naphta remark that his desire for the destruction of Austria is so strong that he is willing for it to arrive "if not on the wings of doves, then on the pinions of eagles." Yet such a desire fits badly with the pedagogue's membership in the various pacifist groups to which he belongs, nor can it really be a part of his grand enterprise to combat "human suffering by the available social methods, to the end of finally eliminating it altogether," in the service of which he is contributing a summary of all literary works concerned with suffering to a forthcoming *Sociology of Suffering*.

Settembrini's platform seems to have been described by Nietzsche thirty-eight years before the publication of *The Magic Mountain* when he wrote of

> the *levelers*—these falsely so-called "free spirits" . . . eloquent and prolifically scribbling slaves of the democratic taste and its "modern ideas" . . . clumsy good fellows whom one should not deny either courage or respectable decency—only they are unfree and ridiculously superficial, above all in their basic inclination to find in the forms of the old society as it has existed so far just about the cause of all human misery and failure . . . what they would like to strive for with all their powers is the universal green-pasture happiness of the herd . . . the two songs and doctrines they repeat most often are "equality of rights" and "sympathy for all that suffers"—and suffering itself they take for something that must be abolished.

The similarities, it seems to me, are too close to be accidental. And the parallel is even deeper, and illuminates not only Settembrini but also some of the other characters and ultimately Hans Castorp himself.

Settembrini is an avowed humanist, a rationalist, a pacifist, an advocate of progress and of the life of practical action. But we have seen that his views are quite inconsistent, his commitment to them ambiguous, and his retreat from the world of action as much a matter of choice as a necessity imposed by his health. Could this be evidence that his "commitment to rationality and enlightenment originate in fear of their opposites, that is to say in a *reactive* emotion, so that his apparently firm and positive intellectual position would in reality rest on literally trembling foundations?" R. J. Hollingdale, who asks that question, gives it a tentatively affirmative answer, mostly on the evidence that Settembrini's characterization eventually turns "frankly into caricature and farce." Furthermore, because Hollingdale accepts the model of dual opposition which we discussed earlier, he is forced to conclude that what Settembrini fears—his wild, sensual, irrational nature—is personified by Naphta, who acknowledges its reality and is unwilling to cover it up with the intellectual machinery which the humanist develops for that purpose.

Settembrini's attitude is indeed reactive, but the evidence for it does not lie in the exaggerations to which he, no less than Naphta, is increasingly prone. Nor is the little half-Jesuit any less self-deceived than the expansive humanist; both of them are equally afraid, and both of them are eagerly covering up what they are afraid of. The evidence for

Settembrini's attitude consists in the very ambiguities in his position which we have been discussing, in the *guazzabuglio* of the ideas he accepts and of the patterns of behavior he exhibits.

Like his grandfather, who was always dressed in black, Settembrini is mourning for the evil present. But the humanist, rationalist, utopian tradition to which he is heir is incapable of providing the solutions he seeks. This tradition is intent on eliminating those very "instinctive," "lower," "animal" traits which, despite his efforts, always make themselves obvious in his behavior. His illness turns out to be the direct result of his inability to fit in the world below and to fight for the cause which he has, consciously or not, begun to suspect. His refusal to leave the Berghof, and his insistence that his case is different from Castorp's, is the result of a prolonged act of self-deception. It manifests his fear that if he does return to the flat-land, where his views are going to be put to the test, his theories will reveal themselves to be useless and he will be unable to control the desires which he is trying to suppress.

Forced by a conflict he observes in himself, Settembrini raises the opposition between animal and human, body and mind, instinct and reason, to a metaphysical principle, and fails to see the continuity between them, the fact that "consciousness is the last and latest development of the organic." In contrast, Hans sees this point clearly when he learns that Joachim's rebellion against Behrens has failed, and that a relapse is forcing him to return post-haste to the Berghof:

> That is serious. And directly before the maneuvers he has been so on fire to go to . . . the body triumphs, it wants something different from the soul, and puts it through—a slap in the face of all those lofty-minded people who think that the body is subordinate to the soul. . . . The question I raise is how far they are right when they set the two over against each other; and whether they aren't rather in collusion, playing the same game.

Does Joachim, Hans is asking, really want to go to the maneuvers as he says he does? Or could the memory of a beautiful patient at the Berghof underlie the flaring up of his illness? "Not that I am for a moment saying anything against Joachim and his 'doggedness'. He is the soul of honour—but what is honour, is what I want to know, when body and soul act together? Is it possible that you have not been able to forget a certain refreshing perfume, a tendency to giggle, a swelling bosom, all waiting for you at Frau Stöhr's table?"

Not seeing that reason is "an instrument of [the] body," Settembrini is afraid of the irrational aspects he finds in himself, which his metaphysics has taught him to consider (if only to avoid responsibility for them) as foreign, and to suppress which he has raised the banner of reason and enlightenment. But his suspicion that *his* reason, at least, cannot combat *his* instincts forces him to avoid the confrontation and to remain inactive on the mountain. Even when the war that was finally to destroy Austria is declared, he deceives himself into remaining at Davos: he continues to perform half-actions, devoting "the remnants of [his] powers to incite [his] country to fight where the spirit and *sacro egoismo* point the way." It is unlikely that his incitements influenced history.

We have seen that Hollingdale finds Settembrini to be reacting to that for which Naphta speaks, "the real world of passion and error." Hollingdale detects here the influence of the young Nietzsche who, under the influence of Schopenhauer, had distinguished between the "real truth of nature and the lie of culture that poses as if it were the only reality." But we have already found in the novel echoes of the later Nietzsche, the author who exposes the "real" world as an error, and asks: "The true world—we have abolished. What world has remained? The apparent one perhaps? But no! With the true world we have also abolished the apparent one."

The novel itself attributes to Naphta the same ambiguous and in-consistent character which we have found in Settembrini. The son of a Jewish ritual butcher, he not only converts to Catholicism, but joins the Society of Jesus. A great dialectician, he argues elegantly and acutely in favor of mysticism and illiteracy. He advocates the suppression of "the rebellion of the flesh," declares himself an enemy of all "worldly things," and scoffs at Settembrini for his "dependence upon bodily comfort." Yet Settembrini is correct in calling him a "voluptuary." His suit is "quiet but modern," his overcoat is lined with fur, his spring coat "looked almost foppish." The luxury of his apartment astonishes the cousins: "there was too much silk about." He takes an elegant tea, and we find him having wine and cake at a cafe where Settembrini is only drinking sugar water. Not only his habits but his very views are inconsistent and paradoxical. He is a "reactionary revolutionist," combining Catholicism and Marxism as easily as Settembrini advocates internationalism and the destruction of Austria. Like Settembrini, he has an answer for every question Hans Castorp is ever likely to ask, and is more than eager to give it. And, also like Settembrini, he is ill.

What brought his illness about and thus prevented Naphta from fulfilling the great expectations he once generated? Despite his happiness in the Jesuit school where he was educated, his "health suffered; less, indeed through the severity of the novitiate . . . than from within." His spirit and his body were restless, incapable of tranquility, a state which seemed to him "a complete atrophy of the personality . . . to which he could never attain, even by the route of physical decay." Nevertheless, he zealously defends that route: "all progress, in so far as there was such a thing, was due to illness. . . . Men consciously and voluntarily descended into disease and madness, in search of knowledge which, acquired by fanaticism, would lead back to health . . ." Yet his admiration for illness is as hollow as Settembrini's contempt for it. Hans knows that Naphta will never be healthy again: " 'Aha!' thought Hans Castorp. 'You unorthodox Jesuit, you with your interpretations of the Crucifixion! It's plain why you never became a priest, *joli jesuite à la petite tache humide!*' " Like Settembrini, Naphta can accept neither the world nor himself. His "moist spot," his illness, allows him to withdraw from both and to maintain an ambiguous alliance to a spirit which delights in sensuality while indulging a body with emasculated desires.

Naphta's express hatred of the physical, but his tacit, if stunted, delight in it, his fundamental ambiguity, recalls the following passage from *The Genealogy of Morals:*

> An ascetic life is a self-contradiction: here rules a *ressentiment* without equal, that of an insatiable instinct and power-will that wants to become master not over something in life but over life itself, over its most profound, powerful, and basic conditions; here an attempt is made to employ force to block up force; here physiological well being itself is viewed askance, and especially the outward expression of this well being, beauty and joy; while pleasure is felt and *sought* in ill-constitutedness, decay, pain, mischance, ugliness, voluntary deprivation, self-mortification, self-flagellation, self-sacrifice. All this is in the highest degree paradoxical: we stand before a discord that *wants* to be discordant, that *enjoys* itself in this suffering and even grows more self-confident and triumphant the more its own presupposition, its physiological capacity for life, decreases.

Naphta, whose ideal is described as "die Askesis," also employs human capacities to combat human capacities; he, too, enjoys illness and decline and distrusts a healthy constitution. But, like Settembrini, his commitment is incomplete. He admires disease and disowns life, but remains on the mountain to preserve his health and to postpone his death. He uses reason to demonstrate reason's inadequacy, and hates to lose an argument. He admires works of art for being ugly and deformed, and praises self-flagellation while sipping tea on his silk sofa.

Neither Naphta nor Settembrini has a hold on reality. Structurally, their views are identical. Both see the world as a battlefield of opposing forces, and each allies himself with the force which leads away from what he considers as low, material, or animal. Settembrini calls that force "reason," while Naphta calls it "faith," but it leads away from the same thing. Neither of them can accept his own sensuality, and each develops a metaphysics to convince himself that that sensuality is not part of his nature. Yet what they oppose is part of themselves and their vague understanding that to accept their view is to deny themselves results in their paradox and, indeed, in their illness, which excuses them from putting their view to the test. Despite their many differences, the two dualistic pedagogues are fleeing the same enemy, and ultimately take the same direction: they both reach the same spot on the magic mountain.

Settembrini idolizes the *homo humanus*, while Naphta advocates the *homo dei*. Such ideals lead away from a reality, and a task, which neither pedagogue is willing to acknowledge. This task, which is again described by Nietzsche, is to

> translate man back into nature; to become master over the many vain and overly enthusiastic interpretations and connotations that have so far been scrawled and painted over that eternal basic text of *homo natura*; to see to it that man henceforth stands before man as even today, hardened in the discipline of science, he stands before the *rest* of nature ... deaf to the siren songs of old metaphysical bird catchers who have been piping at him all too long, "you are more, you are higher, you are of a different origin!"

Even Nietzsche's allusion to the "metaphysical bird catchers" (*metaphysische Vogelfänger*) is echoed in *The Magic Mountain*, since Settembrini introduces himself to Hans with the words of the bird catcher in *The Magic Flute*, Papageno: "Der Vogelfänger bin ich ja, stets lustig, heisa, hopsassa!" Mann's pedagogues both want to believe that they are "more" or "higher" than they are. But one cannot escape what one is, and both end up, ill, on the mountain.

Though this dualistic mold may not fit all the main characters of the novel, it is clear that none of them is simply a "representative" of a particular attitude toward life. The characters do not just represent science or religion, reason or feeling. As we have seen in the case of Settembrini and Naphta, they represent these as specific attempts to escape from what they perceive human nature to be, and of which they are afraid.

Nietzsche's Socrates, who espouses rationality out of a fear of his own instincts, is the paradigmatic reactive character of whom Mann's heroes are variations. By contrast, Hans Castorp appears to be a character Nietzsche might have admired. Consider, for example, Hans's "experimentalism," his willingness to try on new ways and new ideas. This attitude, expressed by the slogan "placet experiri," distinguishes the novel's hero from his various mentors, for they have already decided what is good and what is evil and are thus insensible to new ideas: "*Truthfulness*—I favor any *skepsis* to which I may reply: 'Let us try it.' But I no longer wish to hear anything of all those things and questions that do not permit any experiment. This is the limit of my 'truthfulness'; for there courage has lost its right." Nietzsche here anticipates his later denial of the existence of a final, complete, "objectively" valid picture of the world, or of anything within it. To experiment is here to want to produce and accept only what is likely to lead to fruitful new ideas, some of which may even undermine what led to their acceptance in the first place. This is just the experimentalism which leads Hans Castorp to the intellectual, emotional, and moral adventures he pursues on the mountain. In this he may well belong to "these philosophers of the future [who] may have a right . . . to be called attempters." It is this attitude which makes him see what Settembrini tells him as "not precisely overwhelming, of a value largely experimental, but still worth listening to." Similarly, the pleasure he derives from visiting, against all rules, the terminally ill "was rooted in a tradition diametrically opposed to the one Herr Settembrini, as pedagogue, represented—yet seemed to him, young Hans Castorp, not unworthy of having applied to it the *placet experiri*." Even his participation in the séance in which Joachim appears is motivated by this " 'placet experiri' planted in Hans Castorp's mind by one who would surely and resoundingly have reprobated any experimentation at all in this field."

What is the source of Hans Castorp's experimentalism? Why is he always involved in dubious mental adventures? Though the narrator often reminds us that Hans is in no way "remarkable," he also tells us that many things make him "interesting," one of them his aversion to strain: ". . . he positively saw no reason, or, more precisely, saw no positive reason, for exertion. This then, perhaps, is why we may not call him mediocre: that, somehow or other, he was aware of the lack of such a reason." Hans's awareness that there is no overarching reason for which to live, which is ultimately the cause for the interest his pedagogues show in him, is expressed in the "sympathy with death" which he exhibits from his childhood. Unlike his companions, he refuses to make up such a reason, and this both depends on, and encourages, his experimentalism. Not having made up his mind, he has little to lose. Not thinking that anything is bound to be true, he does not believe that anything is certain to be false. His nature is indeed in this respect "exposed," and Settembrini is right to call him "Life's problem-child."

Hans's illness, like the others', expresses his inability to go on with the life which the flat-land, the practical world for which he has prepared, is offering him. But, unlike the others, he lets his illness take its course while he learns about himself in order to understand what prompted it in the first place. And, alone among his companions, he finds out: ". . . I

have a quarrel after all, not with Clawdia, not with you, Mynheer Peeperkorn, but with my lot in general, my destiny." He alone realizes that
one can only react to the illness by "getting used to not getting used to
it," by not making up one's mind either that one is ill and therefore
bound to remain on the mountain or that the illness does not matter and
that therefore one is obliged to return to the flat-land. He alone refuses
to follow a path dictated either by tradition or by duty, and realizes that,
quite strictly, and despite Settembrini's claims to the contrary, he is a
"still unwritten page."

A quarrel with one's destiny needs to be explained, and if one cannot
question one's destiny, one will find that explanation within oneself.
Unable to accept his lot, but also unable to turn his back to it, Naphta
accounts for his weakness by his materiality, which he turns into a
punishment to which all human beings are subject. Yet in turning against
himself he manages, by a peculiar inversion, to remain at peace with
himself, since he now has an explanation for his suffering, and "the
meaninglessness of suffering, not suffering itself" is what is intolerable.
Settembrini is blithely and self-deceptively convinced that suffering will
be eliminated through progress; Naphta considers it a part of what it is
to be human, and in the comfort he derives from it, he again recalls
Nietzsche's ascetic priest: "It must be a necessity of the first order that
again and again promotes the growth of prosperity of this life-inimical
(*lebensfeindlich*) species—it must indeed be in the interest of life itself
that such a self-contradictory type does not die out."

Unlike his companions, Hans does not take such a stand. He winds
his own phlegmatic way around and between theirs, never quite accepting
but never quite rejecting what they have to offer him. He often enough
speaks in the manner of his friends, but always there is a slight difference.
"You talk about humanity just like Settembrini," Joachim once remarks,
and Hans replies, "Yes—and yet not just the same, either. You have to
take humanity as it is—but even so I find it magnificent." What he finds
magnificent is not, of course, the very vulgarity of Frau Stöhr, the madness
of Lawyer Paravant, or the stupid bravado of Herr Albin, but the mechanism which produces such specimens as solutions to the quarrel with
one's destiny with which he himself is confronted.

It would be wrong to think of Hans Castorp as a model human
character, for Mann's ironic temper precludes such a straightforward
judgment. Hans can deceive himself, for example, as readily as any other
character in the novel. He looks at the back of Clawdia's neck during
Krokowski's lecture just in the manner in which the disgusting Wehsal
stares at the neck of fat Frau Salomon. He gobbles his food down with
the same immense appetite which so shocked him in the other patients

upon his arrival. He does sneak into Clawdia's room after hours to engage in what may well appear to a third party as a sordid little affair. He plays solitaire with the abandon which Lawyer Paravant exhibits in trying to square the circle.

As the novel progresses, the distance between the reader and Hans Castorp constantly increases. After Clawdia's second departure from the Berghof, for example, his own behavior comes to be described almost completely from a third-person point of view, and he is hardly quoted any longer. Accordingly, his state of mind during the last part of his stay and, in particular, the motives of his departure from the Berghof remain a matter for guessing on our part. There is thus always the possibility that Hans is not, after all, so different from the other characters. But because he thinks of himself as such, and because for so much of the novel his point of view is deliberately confused with that of the narrator, whom one expects to be "objective," we may be convinced, for just that reason, that he really is different from the rest. But having noticed that he, too, can deceive himself, we may find the suspicion that he is like the rest impossible to resist. The ease with which he forgets his vision in the snow may support this negative view.

Still, there is no irony in the following statement, which the narrator makes in parting with his hero:

> The young man had indeed, in a stock-taking way, preoccupied himself with this or that among the subjective shadows of things; but the things themselves he had heeded not at all, having a willful tendency to take the shadow for the substance, and in the substance to see only shadow. For this, however, we must not judge him harshly, since the relation between substance and shadow has never been defined once and for all.

Nietzsche once asked about "the apparent *objective* character of things: could it not be merely a difference of degree within the subjective?" Just such doubts prompted Hans Castorp not to take substance for granted, and thus not to think that the value and justification of his life were independently given to him. He tried, while he was on the magic mountain, to find his own. Even if he did succeed, he probably did not succeed on a grand scale, as his unobtrusive departure and his undistinguished march through the battlefields of the War suggest. But then, this metaphysical romance intimates, the grand scale often makes its pursuers ridiculous. For, to quote Nietzsche once again: "It is a measure of the degree of strength of will to what extent one can do without meaning in things, to what extent one can endure to live in a meaningless world because one organizes a small portion of it oneself." The small part of the world which Hans Castorp himself organized *is* himself. And having done that, he goes on to his no longer necessarily interesting fate.

Chronology

1875	Thomas Mann born in Lübeck on June 6 to Senator Johann Heinrich Mann, a merchant, and Julia da Silva-Bruhns Mann.
1890	Senator Mann dies, and the family firm, in which Thomas intended to work, is liquidated.
1893	Mann family moves to Munich; Thomas first works as unpaid apprentice clerk in a fire-insurance company, then becomes part-time student at Munich University.
1894	First short stories published; well received by poet Richard Dehmel.
1896–98	Lives in Italy, mainly with his elder brother, a writer. From 1897 on, works on the editorial staff of satiric magazine *Simplizissimus*, where he publishes some of his short stories.
1898	Publishes *Little Herr Friedemann*, a collection of short novels.
1900	Military service.
1901	Publishes *Buddenbrooks*.
1903	Publishes *Tristan*, a collection of short novels which includes "Tonio Kröger."
1905	Marries Katja Pringsheim, the musical daughter of a well-to-do Jewish University professor. Publishes *Fiorenza*, a Renaissance drama.
1906	Prepares to publish short story, "The Blood of the Volsungs," but withdraws it after his father-in-law objects to its autobiographical detail. Birth of the eldest of his six children, Klaus Heinrich. (The others are Erika, Golo, Monika, Michael, and Elisabeth.)
1909	Publishes *Royal Highness*, a novel.
1910	Suicide of Mann's sister Carla. He begins work on *Felix Krull* (never completed).
1912	Publishes *Death in Venice*. Wife goes to sanatorium in Davos to convalesce after suffering spot on her lung; Mann visits her there.
1918	*Reflections of a Nonpolitical Man* published.
1922	Delivers address to German students, "The German Republic."

1924	Publishes *The Magic Mountain*.
1925	Publishes short novel, *Disorder and Early Sorrow*.
1926	Publishes *Account of My Stay in Paris*, describing one of the many European lecture tours he made during the years of the Weimar Republic.
1929	Awarded Nobel Prize, largely for *Buddenbrooks*.
1930	Publishes *Mario and the Magician*.
1933	Emigrates to Switzerland. Publishes *The Tales of Jacob*, the first volume in the tetralogy *Joseph and His Brothers*.
1934	Publishes *The Young Joseph*, the second volume of *Joseph*.
1935	Publishes volume of essays, *Suffering and Greatness of the Masters*.
1936	Publishes *Joseph in Egypt*, volume three of the *Joseph* tetralogy. Is deprived of his German citizenship, and stripped of his honorary degree from the University of Bonn at Hitler's instigation.
1938	Moves to the United States, living first in Princeton, and then in Pacific Palisades, California.
1939–40	Publishes novel, *The Beloved Returns: Lotte in Weimar*.
1943	Completes *Joseph* tetralogy; publishes *Joseph the Provider*.
1944	Becomes an American citizen.
1947	Publishes *Doktor Faustus*.
1949	Visits Germany to take part in the celebrations of the 200th anniversary of Goethe's birth. Son Klaus commits suicide in Cannes.
1951	Publishes *The Holy Sinner*, a short novel.
1952	Leaves the United States, in part because of the political climate (success of McCarthyism), and settles in Kilchberg, near Zurich.
1953	Publishes *The Black Swan*.
1954	Publishes *Confessions of Felix Krull, Confidence Man*, Part I. Versions of this novel have previously been published in 1922 and 1936.
1955	Publishes *Essay on Schiller*. Dies on August 12 in Zurich.

Contributors

Harold Bloom, Sterling Professor of the Humanities at Yale University, is the author of *The Anxiety of Influence, Poetry and Repression,* and many other volumes of literary criticism. His forthcoming study, *Freud: Transference and Authority,* attempts a full-scale reading of all of Freud's major writings. A MacArthur Prize Fellow, he is the general editor of the Chelsea House Library of Literary Criticism.

Hermann J. Weigand is Sterling Professor of German Literature Emeritus at Yale University. He is the author of *Thomas Mann's Novel "Der Zauberberg": A Study.*

Erich Heller is Professor of German Emeritus at Northwestern University. His books include *The Disinherited Mind* and a study of Thomas Mann.

Georg Lukács was one of the leading European literary critics of this century. He was much involved in Marxist thought and politics in Hungary and elsewhere. His books include *History and Class Consciousness, Essays on Realism,* and *Theory of the Novel.*

C. E. Williams teaches German at the University of East Anglia.

T. J. Reed is Lecturer in German at Oxford University.

W. H. Bruford is Schröder Professor of German Emeritus at Cambridge University.

Henry Hatfield is Senior Research Professor at Harvard University. He is the author of *Crisis and Continuity in Modern German Fiction* and *Goethe: A Critical Introduction.*

Alexander Nehamas is Associate Professor of Philosophy at the University of Pittsburgh.

Bibliography

Bauer, Arnold. *Thomas Mann*. Translated by Alexander and Elizabeth Henderson. New York: Frederick Ungar Publishing Co., Inc., 1971.

Braverman, Albert S. and Larry Nachman. "Nature and the Moral Order in *The Magic Mountain.*" *The Germanic Review*, LIII, no. 1 (1978), 1–12.

Bruford, W. H. *The German Tradition of Self-Cultivation: "Bildung" From Humboldt to Thomas Mann*. Cambridge: Cambridge University Press, 1975.

Bulhof, Francis. "Zauberberg, Magic Mountain, Toverberg." *Babel*, XXI, no. 4 (1975), 173–179.

Bürgin, Hans and Hans-Otto Mayer. *Thomas Mann: A Chronicle of His Life*. Rev. ed., translated by Eugene Dobson. University, Ala.: University of Alabama Press, 1969.

Feuerlicht, Ignace. *Thomas Mann*. New York: Twayne Publishers, Inc., 1968.

Gronicka, André von. *Thomas Mann: Profile and Perspectives*. New York: Random House, 1970.

Hatfield, Henry. *From "The Magic Mountain": Mann's Later Masterpieces*. Ithaca and London: Cornell University Press, 1979.

———. *Thomas Mann: An Introduction to His Fiction*. Rev. ed. New York: New Directions Paperbook, 1962.

———, editor. *Thomas Mann: A Collection of Critical Essays*. Englewood Cliffs, N.J.: Prentice-Hall, Inc., 1964.

Heller, Erich. *The Ironic German: A Study of Thomas Mann*. Boston and Toronto: Little, Brown and Co., 1958.

Hollingdale, R. J. *Thomas Mann: A Critical Study*. Lewisburg, Pa.: Bucknell University Press, 1971.

Jonas, Klaus W. *Fifty Years of Thomas Mann Studies: A Bibliography of Criticism*. Minneapolis: University of Minnesota Press, 1955.

——— and Ilsedore B. Jonas. *Thomas Mann Studies*, Volume 2: *A Bibliography of Criticism*. Philadelphia: University of Pennsylvania Press, 1967.

Kahler, Erich. *The Orbit of Thomas Mann*. Princeton: Princeton University Press, 1969.

Kaufmann, Fritz. *Thomas Mann: The World as Will and Representation*. Boston: Beacon Press, 1957.

Langer, Lawrence L. *The Age of Atrocity: Death in Modern Literature*. Boston: Beacon Press, 1978.

Latta, Alan D. "The Mystery of Life: A Theme in *Der Zauberberg.*" *Monatshefte*, 66, no. 1(1974), 19–32.

Lukács, Georg. *Essays on Thomas Mann*. Translated by Stanley Mitchell. New York: Grosset & Dunlap, 1965.

Mueller, William R. "Thomas Mann's *The Magic Mountain.*" *Thought*, 49, no. 195 (1974), 419–435.

Neider, Charles, editor. *The Stature of Thomas Mann*. New York: New Directions, 1947.

Reed, T. J. *Thomas Mann: The Uses of Tradition.* Oxford University Press, 1974.

Seidlin, Oskar. "The Lofty Game of Numbers: The Mynheer Peeperkorn Episode in Thomas Mann's *Der Zauberberg.*" *PMLA*, 86, no. 5 (1971), 924–939.

Stern, J. P. *Thomas Mann.* London and New York: Columbia University Press, 1967.

Stirk, S. D. "Gerhart Hauptmann and Mynheer Peeperkorn." *German Life and Letters*, n.s. 5(1952), 162–175.

Swales, Martin. *Thomas Mann: A Study.* Totowa, N.J.: Rowman and Littlefield, 1980.

Thomas, R. Hinton. *Thomas Mann: The Mediation of Art.* Oxford: Oxford University Press, 1956.

Webb, Eugene. *The Dark Dove: The Sacred and Secular in Modern Literature.* Seattle and London: University of Washington Press, 1975.

Weigand, Hermann J. *Thomas Mann's Novel "Der Zauberberg": A Study.* New York: AMS Press, 1971.

Wesche, Ulrich. "Beyond 'Bourgeois Realism': The Grotesque and the Sublime in Thomas Mann's *The Magic Mountain.*" *Denver Quarterly*, 13, no. 2(1978), 81–91.

Yourcenar, Marguerite. "Humanism in Thomas Mann." *Partisan Review.* 23(1956), 153–170.

Acknowledgments

"Disease" by Hermann J. Weigand from *Thomas Mann's Novel "Der Zauberberg": A Study* by Herman J. Weigand, copyright © 1971 by AMS Press. Reprinted by permission.

"Conversation on *The Magic Mountain*" by Erich Heller from *Thomas Mann: The Ironic German* by Erich Heller, copyright © 1958, 1961 by Erich Heller. Reprinted by permission of Meridian/The World Publishing Company.

"In Search of Bourgeois Man" by Georg Lukács from *Essays on Thomas Mann* by Georg Lukács, copyright © 1964 by Merlin Press Ltd. Reprinted by permission of Grosset & Dunlap.

"Not an Inn, But an Hospital" by C. E. Williams from *Forum for Modern Language Studies* by C. E. Williams, copyright © 1973 by University of Saint Andrews, Scotland/Department of French. Reprinted by permission.

"The Uses of Tradition" by T. J. Reed from *Thomas Mann: The Uses of Tradition* by T. J. Reed, copyright © 1974 by Oxford University Press. Reprinted by permission.

" 'Bildung' in *The Magic Mountain*" by W. H. Bruford from *The German Tradition of Self-Cultivation: "Bildung" from Humboldt to Thomas Mann* by W. H. Bruford, copyright © 1975 by Cambridge University Press. Reprinted by permission.

"*The Magic Mountain*" by Henry Hatfield from *From the Magic Mountain: Mann's Later Masterpieces* by Henry Hatfield, copyright © 1979 by Cornell University. Reprinted by permission of Cornell University Press.

"Nietzsche in *The Magic Mountain*" by Alexander Nehamas from *Philosophy and Literature* by Alexander Nehamas, copyright © 1981 by The University of Michigan at Dearborn. Reprinted by permission.

Index